A SHORT
NEWTON
CHESTER

A SHORT HISTORY OF NEWTON HALL, CHESTER

CHRIS FOZZARD

atmosphere press

© 2022 Chris Fozzard

Published by Atmosphere Press

Cover design by Beste Miray

No part of this book may be reproduced without permission from the author except in brief quotations and in reviews.

atmospherepress.com

To the occupants of Newton Hall — past, present and future — all of whom are or will be part of its history

Newton Hall

Contents

Introduction	*iii*
Chapter 1: Early Newton and the Origins of Newton Hall	3
Chapter 2: The Property	30
Chapter 3: The Late Eighteenth and Early Nineteenth Century	39
Chapter 4: The Mid- to Late Nineteenth Century	76
Chapter 5: The Early to Mid-Twentieth Century	103
Chapter 6: The Mid-Twentieth Century to the Present Day	122
Conclusion	129
Illustrations	133
Family Trees	159
Notes and References	175
Sources for Illustrations	183
Index	185

Introduction

In the summer and early autumn of 2016, I was in house-hunting mode. I had rented a house in Upton-by-Chester for a while and had decided it was time to have a place I could call my own. And it was a house that I was hunting, rather than a flat. My initial search did not extend beyond the doorstep of the property I was then inhabiting. I was settled there, it was ample for my purposes, and there was no imperative to leave an area that I had become familiar with and attached to over many years. I called the landlord and made him an offer. He spoke to his wife, they deliberated, and in the end decided for their own good reasons that it was not the right time to sell. After that, I viewed many houses, making an offer on an appealing Victorian terraced property a short distance away from where I then lived, which proved to be abortive. In short, little progress was being made.

In the meantime, a flat in a nearby converted building called Newton Hall, of which I had no prior knowledge given that it is discreetly situated on a private road with no through access, seemed to be appearing in my property searches with a disproportionate and insistent regularity.

Initially, I discarded it as it fell outside my search criteria but, as no more houses caught my eye, I felt there was no harm to be done from a viewing. Driving up the short rise of the tree-lined Newton Hall Drive, flanked by post-war housing on one side and playing fields on the other, I was immediately struck by the building that confronted me. It had a scale and symmetry all of its own and a robust grandeur without a hint of ostentation. It was also improbably old for the area, and that was a large part of its charm. Surely, it had a story or two to tell.

I was escorted through the main front door, beneath an embedded sundial with more than a nod to the Tudor period, and up a broad staircase, complete with warped oak banister. The flat, on the first floor and one of twelve, was bright, airy, and well-proportioned too. It had enough elevation to command fine views to the south and west, mostly of the city of Chester and the Welsh hills beyond. When the sale was completed a few weeks later and I entered the flat unaccompanied for the first time, it felt as though those views belonged exclusively to me. I was equally certain that I was not the first to have experienced that sensation.

As a flat-owner and resident, my interest in the building grew, particularly from a historical perspective. I made enquiries of more established neighbours, but little seemed to be known. Often, they had the same questions as me and were similarly curious for answers. If I were to build up any sort of picture, a research project would be required. I had a modicum of experience and some basic collateral to get me started in this case. I had enjoyed a long and active association with Upton-by-Chester Local History Group and, as a result, had access to a small miscellaneous collection of Newton-related materials in the group's archives.

One item that particularly caught my attention was a laminated estate map of Newton dated 1738. 'Newton Hall and Gardens' (fig. 1) can be made out, along with some barely decipherable footnotes (fig. 2), one of which reads, 'The yellow letters shew Mad^m Hurleston Widow her jointure.' This was my first acquaintance with the Hurleston name. The yellow letters were in and around Newton Hall.

Separately, whilst browsing through a Victorian directory in Chester Reference Library, I came across the following intriguing passage:

> Newton Hall ... is a red brick building, erected about the time of Queen Anne, standing in extensive well-wooded grounds and had originally a moat. Near this hall a battle was fought in the year 1644 between a detachment of the garrison of Chester and Parliamentary forces.[1]

From this we can make some deductions: the age of the building is uncertain, and it is considerably older than may at first be supposed; it was once part of a much larger estate, possibly including defensive earthworks; and it has connections with the English Civil War, which was raging throughout the land in 1644, even though the hall itself may not have existed at that time — Queen Anne reigned from 1702 to 1714.

With this slender detail, I set out to build a deeper and more rounded history of the hall. My browsing at the Reference Library and at Cheshire Archives and Local

Studies became more focused and intense. I consulted, amongst other things, revered old history books (often yellow and brittle with age), long-undisturbed contracts and correspondence, and modern genealogy websites, comparing and corroborating data where I could. I captured notes on spreadsheets, sorted by source and incumbent family, and began compiling the family trees that in their fuller form would find their way into this book. When new locations presented themselves, I visited them when I could, collecting photographs and additional relevant information.

At this point, though, the knowledge was enough for me. I foresaw no body of work sufficient for a publication and time looked like an inhibitor. All that changed when the global pandemic racked the UK from March 2020 onwards. Like many others, my regular sources of work were affected and I had time on my hands. By this stage, my research was gaining heft, raising the possibility of turning the reality of my situation into an unbidden opportunity. I sat at my desk in Newton Hall, ruminating on the view outside, and made the first tentative taps on my keyboard. Still with little idea of where the journey would take me, I continued to peer purblind into the past. What follows is my attempt at explaining what I saw.

1

Early Newton and the Origins of Newton Hall

Settlement in Newton dates back many centuries, belying its name. Place names with the prefix 'new' are commonly ancient in origin as they represent the first instance of habitation in the location. The township was included in the Domesday Hundred of Chester, next to Upton and north-east of the liberties.[1] The holder of the land, which amounted to one hide,[2] was 'Erne of Neston'. By 1086 he had passed the land, together with his holdings in the liberty, to William Fitz Neil, who later gave it to the Abbey of St. Werburgh. Fitz Neil's grant also included the services of Hugh Fitz Ozard, ancestor of the Duttons, who long held lands in Newton. In the early thirteenth century, the township gave its name to a family which had extensive holdings under the abbot. In the later thirteenth and early fourteenth century, the mayoral family of Brickhill also acquired considerable estate in Newton.

There is an old story, of uncertain date and provenance, that the Newton estate was given to the Constable of Chester — of whom there were eleven between the Norman Conquest and the mid-fourteenth century — as a reward for holding back the waters of the River Dee so that a group of Englishmen could escape the clutches of the marauding Welsh. The river long marked the border between England and Wales in the Chester area and was of vital strategic importance. The Old Dee Bridge was built in 1387 — after the title 'Constable of Chester' became extinct — though other forms of crossing pre-dated it, going back to Roman times. There is no obvious connection between the holders of the title and the Newton area or people known to have been active in it through this period, so the story does need to be treated with some caution. There is a more well-founded reference, however, to the medieval lord of the manor, Gui de Nuetone, though again no date. Like many medieval noblemen, he appears to have been of Norman origin and may well have had his manor house on the Newton Hall site.[3]

Despite changes in land ownership in the centuries following the Norman Conquest, the Abbey of St. Werburgh retained strong interests in the Newton area. Upon the Dissolution of the Monasteries under Henry VIII in the late 1530s, the manor passed to the dean and chapter of Chester but was amongst those holdings alienated in the 1550s and, by the 1580s, it was held by the Hurleston family of Picton.[4]

There appear to have been disputes over the land in the wake of the Dissolution involving two notable families: the Cottons and the Grosvenors. Richard Cotton and his elder brother, George, both held important positions at the court of Henry VIII and Richard became Knight of the

Shire of Cheshire in 1554. John and Richard Grosvenor, ancestors of the Dukes of Westminster, were the ones with whom they took issue. Croston tells us that 'eventually the feoffees[5] surrendered to the Crown; on 19 December 1579 the whole of the lands formerly held by the Abbey were granted by Elizabeth [Queen Elizabeth I] to Sir George Calvely, knight, George Cotton, Hugh Cholmondely, Thomas Legh, Henry Mainwaring, John Nuttall and Richard Hurleston esq and their heirs for ever'.[6] Ormerod confirms that the Hurlestons were 'seized of the manor of Newton juxta Chester, and lands therein, and in Upton, Idenshaw, Wirwyn, and Croughton; granted by the queen ... yielding £52 per annum ad part occident ... and of the manor of Hurleton, co Lanc'.[7]

An account passed down the Hurleston family line suggests that there was an opportunist 'land grab' at the time of the Dissolution which was later formalised through a lawsuit. This action, it is postulated, only succeeded because the recipients bribed the judge, the Earl of Leicester.[8]

Whatever the means of acquisition, it is clear that the Hurlestons had become significant landowners based on these holdings in Cheshire and Lancashire and it is to this family that we now more directly turn our attention.

'Hurleston' is an uncommon name, which is always a blessing for the researcher. Set against that, however, is the variability of the spelling, which was characteristic of the time. Variants included 'Hurleton' — as in the place name above — 'Hurlston', 'Hurleston', and 'Hurlstone'. 'Hurlestone' is also widely referenced, including in the modern-day street name, 'Hurlestone Close', in Mickle Trafford, near Chester. 'Hurleston' appears to have become most prevalent and has persisted in the family's genealogy to the present day. There is some evidence that it was pronounced with three syllables with the stress on a short 'e' sound in the second syllable.

The Hurlestons had a long association with the small settlement of Picton, a few miles east of Newton. Their residence was Picton Hall, which Bernard Wall tells us 'began as a manor house in Norman times'.[9] He continues, 'Ormerod provides information on the families who lived there, including the Hurleston family of the 17th century, some of whom are buried in the big vault outside Plemstall Church.' In fact, Richard Hurleston was one of the earliest members of the family to have been connected with Picton, his birth having been recorded there in 1531 (see Family Tree A). His son, John, boasts a great claim to fame as a mariner and associate of Drake and Raleigh, distinguishing himself in the fight against the Spanish Armada in 1588. A stamp issued in 1988 to commemorate the 400th anniversary of its defeat featured his image (fig. 3).[10] When he died in 1593, the list of his estates in his *inquistio post mortem* recorded Newton first and made no mention of Picton at all.[11] This may have been an early indication of Newton's potential become the main family seat, or an expression of gratitude for the bequest from the Queen, who was still on the throne at that time.

There is another intriguing reference to a John Hurleston in Chester in the sixteenth century, though his precise lineage is uncertain. He was Dr. John Hurleston, Carmelite prior of Chester from 1537–1538 — undoubtedly the most eventful time to occupy this position given that it coincided directly with the Dissolution. Some ex-friars found favour under the new regime, regardless of whether they had trimmed their theology to align with it. It is conceivable that this was the case with John Hurleston and that he was influential in the granting of monasterial land to Richard Hurleston in 1579. We know that he survived into the 1570s from this extract from *The Victoria History of the County of Chester*: 'The last prior, John Hurleston, had studied theology at Oxford and Cologne and was described as "a very discreet man" when he offered to act as confessor to Piers Fieldy at his execution in 1573.'[12] Further details of this precise transaction and the circumstances around it are unknown.

John Hurleston, the renowned mariner, was succeeded by two consecutive heirs also named 'John', the first of whom died at the age of seventy-nine in 1669. He had married Anne Wilbraham of Woodhey in 1609. She was born and died in the same years as her husband. Together they had nineteen children, only five of whom outlived their parents, many of them dying at birth. Their son and heir, John, was born in 1618 and died in 1687. This was an eventful period for the nation, the county and the family — politically, militarily and constitutionally. It also led up to the construction of Newton Hall.

In late 1642 the English Civil War erupted, with the first major encounter taking place inconclusively at Edgehill on 23rd October. The following January, Sir Thomas Aston, who had fought at Edgehill on the Royalist side, was appointed by the King as Major-General of Cheshire and Lancashire with instructions to protect the strategically important county of Cheshire from advancing Parliamentary troops under Sir William Brereton. The forces of Brereton and Aston met at the Battle of Middlewich on 13th March 1643, resulting in an overwhelming victory for the Parliamentarians and the capture of more than 400 Royalist soldiers. A contemporary account states, 'We tooke Sir Edward Mosely Baronet, one Colonell, one Sergeant Major, eleven Captaines, 3 of them Cheshire men, Captaine John Hurleston, Cap Massie of Cottington and Cap Starkie ...' This gives us an insight into the status and allegiances of the Hurleston family. Perhaps their support for the King was unsurprising given their connection with Chester and its Royalist stance at that time. Indeed, the King had visited Chester on 26th September 1642 and members of the Hurleston family may well have met him on that occasion.[13]

It is not known exactly what happened to John Hurleston in the wake of his capture but it is possible to speculate based on documented facts. The following entry appears in the *House of Commons Journal* from 28th December 1647:[14]

> Resolved, &c. That this House doth accept of the Sum of Thirteen hundred and Forty Pounds,[15] for a Fine, for the Delinquency of John Hurleston, of Picton in the County of Chester, Esquire; and John Hurleston his Son and Heir Apparent: The Offence of the Father, That he left his own Habitation, and went into and resided in the Enemies Quarters: The Son was in Arms against the Parliament: Rendered in April, 1646; but took the Covenant the Three-and-twentieth of March, 1645 ... An Ordinance for granting a Pardon unto John Hurleston, of Picton in the County of Chester, Esquire, and John Hurleston

his Son, for their Delinquencies, and for taking off the Sequestration of their Estates, was this Day read; and, upon the Question, passed; and ordered to be sent unto the Lords for their Concurrence.

This account strongly suggests that it was the son, born in 1618, who was captured at the Battle of Middlewich, as he was the active soldier, rather than the father, born in 1590. The price of freedom, it seems, was the signing of the Solemn League and Covenant — an undertaking to fight for Parliament — and a heavy fine based on the value of the land owned by the family and associated rents. Despite this, both father and son retained their allegiance to the King and demonstrated this through their actions. Their land, furthermore, was confiscated and only recovered on payment of the fine.

Powerful sentiment ran so strongly against the Hurleston family that, for a time, they were forced to flee to Holland. This would have been regarded as a safe haven because the Dutch were sympathetic to Charles I, not least on account of the fact that his daughter Mary was married to William II, Prince of Orange. Moreover, the King's son, the future Charles II, took refuge there in 1648.

To pay their dues, the Hurlestons sold one of their principal properties, at Iddenshaw near Tarporley. Regrettably, this property no longer exists. It was an astute transaction by John Hurleston, as the purchaser was his son-in-law, Sir Peter Pindar, so the property remained in the family and the charge over their other possessions was lifted.[16] The sale agreement, held at the Cheshire Archives, shows the amount that changed hands to have been £3,500, meaning that considerable additional capital was released to John and his son as a result. The document is dated 21st June 1647 and the purchaser recorded as 'Peter Pindar of Whitby, co. York, gent'. He made his money from the manufacture of alum from shale mined in that part of the world. Alum was a precious commodity, with numerous uses including in the dyeing of textiles, papermaking and cosmetics. Peter had married Dorothy Hurleston in 1638. In 1662, shortly after the Restoration of the Monarchy and most likely as a token of gratitude for his support, he was made first Baronet of Iddenshaw.

Not all delinquent families were fortunate or, perhaps, enterprising enough to recover their possessions. Had the Hurlestons failed in this endeavour, they would not have had the land and resources upon which to build Newton Hall.

As an aside, the date of the above parliamentary discharge is evidence of Puritan repudiation of the festive season.

What can be made, therefore, of the assertion in the directory that 'near this hall a battle was fought in 1644'? From the records, it is certain that there was serious military engagement in the area at the time. Indeed, Chester was directly embroiled in the Civil War before this, suffering its first casualty in July 1643.[17] Defensive earthworks — makeshift walls, trenches and mounts — were hastily constructed from the north-west corner of the city walls, running through Flookersbrook and down to the river, to protect the suburbs to the north and east, which were most vulnerable to attack. In November 1643, Flookersbrook Hall and Bache Hall were burnt to the ground by the Royalist command to prevent them from being occupied as lodgings by opposing forces.[18] A similar local property, Upton Hall, was garrisoned by Brereton's soldiers soon afterwards and there is evidence of fighting in the area in the form of cannon ball finds.[19] Royalist soldiers were billeted at Picton Hall, which also provided stabling for horses and storage and rationing of grain. As we can see, the Hurlestons were taking extreme risks on and beyond the battlefield at this time.

On a broader front, there was a major encounter at Nantwich in January 1644, which resulted in a resounding victory for the Parliamentary forces. The King's nephew, Prince Rupert, arrived in Chester with his troops in March, after a swift campaign through Lancashire and Cheshire, and began to further improve the city's fortifications. After his defeat at Marston Moor near York in July 1644, he fell back on Chester, where raids on the adversary's positions were undertaken by both sides. By this time, Brereton's troops were beginning to encircle the city, advancing from their strongholds further east. The combination of this advance and the Royalist effort to reinforce the city beyond the walls to the east makes it highly likely that conflict took place in and around the Newton area, if not a set-piece battle. The first full-on siege of Chester began in November 1644.

Given the knowledge of the Hurlestons fighting for the King in 1642 and 1646, it is difficult imagine that they were not directly involved in the defence of the city during the great four-month siege that began with the Battle of Rowton Heath in September 1645 and that ended in its capitulation. There is strong circumstantial evidence to that effect through their connections, one of whom was Sir

Geoffrey Shakerley, Lieutenant-Colonel in the King's forces. In later years, Shakerley's daughter, Anne, would marry Charles Hurleston (b 1658) and the couple would inhabit Newton Hall. As Shakerley was a very wealthy man — with property in Lancashire, Cheshire, Berkshire, and London — it is possible that Anne's dowry helped towards the creation of the Newton Hall estate.

Burke describes Geoffrey Shakerley as follows:

> This personage, a staunch and devoted loyalist, suffered severely for his attachment to the Stuarts. He was several times imprisoned and had his lands confiscated. Upon the restoration, however, he obtained restitution and was appointed by the King governor of Chester Castle. In Pennant's Wales is recorded a gallant exploit of this stout cavalier. During the battle between Poyntz and Sir Marmaduke Langdale, on Rowton Heath, Colonel Shakerley was commissioned to carry the intelligence of an advantage of the Royalists to the King, in Chester, then beleaguered, and to avoid a troublesome circuit, he crossed the Dee in a tub, his horse swimming at the side; and offered to carry back the king's commands in a quarter of an hour, in the same manner. Charles delayed, Poyntz rallied and the royal cavalry were destroyed, which put to an end his Majesty's project of joining Montrose, who was then in force in Scotland.[20]

John Barratt adds that Shakerley 'would be an active royalist conspirator throughout the interregnum'.[21] His allegiances and fortunes were not far removed from those of the Hurlestons at this time, which may have created or strengthened the bond between the families.

The Restoration of the Monarchy in 1660 would have re-introduced some stability into lives of the Hurleston family, especially given their long-standing and high-profile Royalist sympathies and network. In the succeeding twenty years or so, we see a number of transactions in the Cheshire Archives suggesting that they were putting their affairs in order by setting up or formalising leases and tenancies on their land. Randle Holme's *Survey of Cheshire* in 1671 records John Hurleston as lord of the manor of Picton and says of Newton-by-Chester, 'Charles Hurlestone holds it in soccage[22] paying yearly [rent] to the Cathedral.' Two facts are of particular interest here: firstly, that the cathedral has retained a claim to the land and, secondly, that John Hurleston and Charles, his son and heir, are identified with separate locations.

Deeper investigation reveals further evidence of the Hurlestons having a concurrent presence in Picton and Newton in the latter part of the seventeenth century. The *inquisitio post mortem* of the John Hurleston who died in 1593 has the Newton and Upton townships comprising eight dwelling-houses, six cottages, a windmill, 300 acres of plough land, 300 acres of pasture, 200 acres of meadow, and 300 acres of heath and moor. However, the first indication of Hurleston residency in Newton comes in 1657. The younger of the two John Hurlestons alive at that time was married at St. Oswald's in Chester, the church of the parish in which Newton then stood. Two years later his son William was baptised at the same place. In 1664 he is referred to as 'John Hurleston of Newton' in the record of his daughter's burial at Plemstall, the parish church which served Picton. In 1669, his father died, apparently triggering a move on his part from Newton to Picton as the new head of the family. We can infer this from lists of Cheshire gentry in the early 1670s, which include 'John Hurleston of Picton, esq'. In the late 1670s and early 1680s we begin to see references to 'Charles Hurleston of Newton' in church records at St. Oswald's. This is the eldest son of John Hurleston, now of Picton. A clear picture is emerging from 1657 onwards of Picton being the grander property, occupied by the head of the family, and an early Newton property being the residence of the eldest son and heir in which to live and raise his own family.

In 1683 a significant change occurred. Charles Hurleston left Newton and went to live in Chester. It is a reasonable assumption that the motive for this was that the new property — Newton Hall — was being built. When it was finished, it seems that the first occupants were Charles's father, whose will of 1687 records him as 'John Hurleston of Newton', and John's wife, Mary. Clearly, Newton Hall was fitter than Picton Hall for the head of the family. Charles remained in Chester for a spell and did not fully establish himself and his family at the hall until after his mother's death in 1693.[23] All of this helps to place the date of construction in the mid-1680s, contradicting entries in nineteenth and twentieth century directories that date it from the reign of Queen Anne.

As was the case with many families during this period, the political and religious affiliations of the Hurlestons appeared to change over time, most likely in response to considerations of safety, security and expedience. Their support for the King during the Civil War suggests leanings towards Catholicism, or at least aversion the brand of Puritan Protestantism practised by powerful republicans. Or they may simply have been toeing the local party line.

The same John Hurleston who fought as a young man for Sir Thomas Aston at Middlewich appears over forty years later in the diary of his son, Sir Willoughby Aston, Sheriff of Cheshire in 1680 and 1690. This time he is supporting the Duke of Monmouth — Charles II's eldest illegitimate son — in his succession claims to rival the future James II, Charles's brother and an avowed Catholic. The Duke of Monmouth had visited Chester, staying with the mayor, George Mainwaring, and attending services at the cathedral. It appears that he was lauded by the local gentry. In 1682, John Hurleston, still of Picton at this time, had to surrender four brace of pistols to the Lord Lieutenant as part of a wider process of disarmament. He may have felt a particular attachment to the cause given his earlier exile in Holland, where the Duke was born and spent his early years.[24] In the end, Monmouth's hopes were extinguished by defeat at the Battle of Sedgemoor in July 1685, shortly after James's accession to the throne.

Writing in September 1688 and reflecting on earlier events, Aston tell us of dissatisfied parties holding 'a public reception and entertainment of the Duke of Monmouth in this countie'. He adds that 'those that harbour and countenance of nonconformist ministers should be obliged to give security of the peace and particularly ... John Hurleston of Newton esq and Charles his son. We also present that those not frequenting church according too law are recusants ...'[25] It is interesting that Aston connects John Hurleston — recently deceased at the time of his writing — with Newton, but not his son. This is further corroborating evidence that John spent his final years at Newton Hall and that Charles was elsewhere.[26] It is also a tantalising conjecture that, amongst the early occupants of the property, were recusant ministers as fugitives from justice. When the hall was converted in the early 1990s, the builders reportedly searched for 'priest holes' in what are now Flats 1 and 2. Nothing was found, possibly because they never existed or possibly because, by their very nature, such features necessitate the utmost in concealment.

Whatever politics the leading members of the Hurleston family espoused at this time, they were still subject to the strictures of the law of the land and the demands of powerful local forces answerable to the King. The following is an extract from a call to arms of 1683, issued by the Deputy Lieutenants of Cheshire to certain landowners to provide military aid to Sir Philip Egerton, Member of Parliament (MP) for Cheshire since 1681, a Catholic and supporter of James II.

> Whereas the Ho'ble the De; Leiuf'ts of this county of Chester haue appoynted S'r Peter Pindar, Barr'tt, and JOHN HURLESTON, Esq. who have hereunto Subscribed Our Names, to find a militia horse with arms and all other ffurniture for horse and Man, a horse Man's Coate, poud'r and Bullett, and all other things as by Law Required, to Ride in the Troope of Sir Phillip Egerton, Kn't, Wee doe hereby declare our submission thereunto, and for the better performance thereof have agreed and hereby doe Covenant and agree that Henceforth the s'd S'r Peter Pyndar shall, from time to time when Legally therevnto required, pay such Rider such daily pay, and pouder

and Bullett, as by law directed. And that the sayed JOHN HURLESTON, Esqr., shall at all times and as often as lawfully therevnto Required finde a Suffitient horse and Ryder with all sorts of Armes and furniture with horseman's Coate and what elce the s'd Dep: Leif'ts shall require and appoynt. Wittnesse Our hands and Seales the Sixth day of June, An'o Dom'i 1683.[27]

If it were the case that John Hurleston's sympathies were with the Duke of Monmouth at the time, then this communication would have been very ill-received. Whatever the fact of the matter, it is unlikely that there would have been any material call on his resources given the Duke's somewhat lame and abortive attempted coup two years later.

The wider religious commitment and conformity of the Hurleston family is not in question. They are closely associated with and, in their time, were considerable benefactors towards St. Peter's Church, Plemstall (fig. 4). This church, located on a site where worship has taken place for over a thousand years, is less than a mile away from the former family seat at Picton Hall. Even in the religiously turbulent times following the Restoration they were making donations to the church. *The Cheshire Sheaf* talks of 'Gifts to the Poore and Schoole ye parish of Plemstone since ye year 1660' and states, 'Anne Hurlestone, wife of John Hurlestone esq of Pickton, gave a broadcloth communion table with a cushin and a pulpit cloth.'[28] There is also a substantial family vault at the rear of the church, as mentioned by Wall and to which we shall return shortly.

In 1678, the marriage took place between Charles Hurleston and Anne Shakerley (see Family Tree B), whose father by then was Governor of Chester Castle. The *Victoria History of the County of Chester* tells us:

> In 1680 the Governor, Geoffrey Shakerley, was ordered to disband the foot company garrisoning the castle and, by 1681, there remained only 3 gunners. At the time of the Duke of Monmouth's visit in 1682 its undefended state caused the government alarm.

It is unclear from whom the order came and what the purpose was. Given the level of support for the Duke in Chester, it may well have been strategically rather than financially motivated. Ormerod's genealogy of the Hurlestons indicates that Charles and Anne had twelve children between 1683 and 1704, of whom only two — John and another Charles — appear to have survived infancy.

More evidence of the wealth and standing of the Hurlestons — and their continued involvement in constitutional debate — comes at the time of the Jacobite Rising in 1715. Charles Hurleston — the younger of the two brothers just mentioned — was involved in a gentlemen's club with eminent Cheshire nobles who met to discuss the claims of the Old Pretender, James Francis Edward Stuart — son of James II — and whether to support them. Crossley in his history *Cheshire* provides the following wry account:

> The last and fifth in descent [of the Breretons] built a domestic chapel at Ashley Hall and a dining hall in 1653. In 1715 it was hung with the portraits of the ten gentlemen who met there to discuss a Stuart rising.

Fortunately for themselves they decided finally by a casting vote to support the reigning monarch and, when things went ill with the Stuart claims, they commemorated their unanimous decision by having their portraits painted and hung in the dining hall. These portraits included those of Asherton of Ashley, Sir Richard Grosvenor of Eaton, James, Earl Barrymore of Marbury, Charles Hurleston of Newton [fig. 5], Amos Meredith of Henbury, John Warren of Poynton, Henry Legh and Peter Legh of Lymm. The paintings are supposed to be hung at Tatton Hall, Ashley Hall being reduced to a farmhouse.[29]

On this occasion, the Hurlestons and their confederates backed a winner, but only just. It is worth adding that Charles Hurleston was not the head of the family at this time. That was his brother, John, who died at Newton Hall at the age of thirty-five in 1720. It is possible that he was physically incapacitated — although he did father seven children between 1706 and 1713 — or perhaps he was simply disinclined. *The Cheshire Sheaf* makes reference to a James Bennett of Newton, Yeoman and tenant of the Hurlestons, who refused to sign the Oath of Allegiance to George I in 1714–1715 and was declared 'a Papist'.[30] He is compared to Charles Hurleston in that he also did not go so far as to join 'that ill-starred outbreak' and take arms against his King.

Two of John's children were sons, who, along with one of his daughters, predeceased him. His younger brother, Charles, therefore did become head of the family on his death in 1720. A monumental inscription (fig. 6) on the south wall inside St. Peter's Church, Plemstall, captures the recent history of the main line of the Hurlestons of Newton at this time:

> Underneath lie interred John Hurlestone of Picton esq and Anne his wife, Daughter of Thomas Wilbraham of Woodhey in this county. Here also lie Charles Hurlestone esq, their son and heir, and his wife, Daughter of Jeffrey Shakerley of Hulme in this county kt. Underneath also lies John Hurlestone of Newton near Chester esq Son and heir of the above mentioned Charles and Anne who died 12 August 1720. He left issue by Mary his Relict, eldest daughter of Sir John Williams of Pengethley in the county of Hereford, kt and Bart. 4 daughters: Anne, Mary, Penelope and Elizabeth.[31]

John's marriage to Mary is further evidence of the Hurlestons' propensity to marry into titled families.

Charles married Elizabeth Lander of Shrigley in 1723 and the pressure was on to produce a male heir to preserve the family line. Tragically, Elizabeth died four years later, leaving Charles a childless widower. Above the Hurleston family vault, immediately to the rear of St. Peter's Church, is a tablet (fig. 7) with its wording almost completely obliterated by weathering but known to have poignantly commemorated a 'young wife' who was 'beautiful in her person, discreet in her behaviour, a dutiful daughter, an observant wife, and had she lived a few weeks longer might have been a happy mother'.[32] It appears that Elizabeth was in the advanced stages of pregnancy when she passed away.

The inscription begins: 'In this vault lies the body of Elizabeth, wife of Charles Hurleston, of Newton esq, youngest daughter and coheir of Thomas Lander, of Newhall, in the County of Lancaster, esq, by Elizabeth, daughter of Edward Downes, of Shrigley, in the county of Chester, esq.' The wording is not lengthy but it goes back two generations to make explicit mention of Edward Downes, Elizabeth's maternal grandfather. This implies a strong connection between the Hurleston and Downes families. Edward Downes's son and Elizabeth's uncle, also Edward, was High Sheriff of Cheshire in 1723 and 1724. Charles Hurleston himself attained this coveted position in November 1726, his wife dying almost at the end of his tenure in December of the following year. It would have been a doleful and chill procession indeed, making its way across country from Newton Hall to Plemstall for Elizabeth's funeral and interment.

The tablet also bears the Hurleston family crest (fig. 8), which includes four 'ermine spots' — black arrows with three dots at their tip to mimic markings on the winter coat of the ermine or stoat. This is a common motif in heraldry. Ermine is a regal fur, which has long been associated with the crowns and robes of royal and noble people. It symbolises valour, justice and dignity. Perhaps this provides some insight into the values and aspirations of the Hurleston family. One present-day legacy of the crest is Ermine Road at Flookersbrook, which once occupied Hurleston land.

The vault itself is impressive in its scale and thought-provoking for the motifs it bears (figs. 9 and 10). A raised sarcophagus carries the images of almost life-size skeletons on either side. They are not quite identical, as the one on the north elevation has more ribs, which could signify a female, based on the biblical account of Adam donating a rib for the creation of Eve. This figure is holding up and contemplating an hourglass, whilst in the other hand there appears an arrow pointed at the midriff. The skeleton on the south elevation is holding the stem of an arrow in a posture suggesting it is about to pierce the upper body. In the other hand are acanthus leaves, which also appear on the east and west ends of the sarcophagus. It has been suggested that the symbolism here is primarily biblical with generalised representations of mortality.[33] However, knowledge of the Hurleston family and its demise permits a more personal and literal interpretation. The fact that Elizabeth Hurleston's memorial tablet is placed immediately above the tomb raises the probability that Charles added the sarcophagus at the same time. The hourglass could therefore represent Elizabeth's untimely death and the arrow pointing to the womb the same fate befalling her unborn child. On the other skeleton, an arrow to the heart may represent the effect of those losses on Charles or the futility of his life thereafter. Whilst open to other interpretations, there are heavy overtones of self-harm, including with the leaves, which may hint at guilt and a desire for expiation. Whatever its meaning, the imagery is macabre, stark and unprepossessing. Even today, the vault faces out onto the flat, bleak Gowy marshes, evoking a sense of wistfulness and desolation.

On 19th April 1729, Charles remarried. His wife on this occasion was Susannah Piggot, with the wedding taking place at Hodnet in Shropshire. She, we are told, was the eighth child of 'Robert Piggot, servant and friend of the House of Grosvenor'.[34] It appears that this union was also without issue.

The Hurleston line was fleetingly maintained by the

surviving children of Charles's brother John (see Family Tree C). This was an eventful period for that branch of the family. John and his wife, Mary, married at Newton Hall in 1705 and had their seven children there. The two sons — another John and Charles — died in infancy, as mentioned, in 1706 and 1711 respectively. The eldest daughter, Jane, died in 1718 at the age of ten and another daughter, Penelope, at the age of eleven in 1723, the same year as her mother.

Childlessness, high infant-mortality and premature death were characteristic of the time. What may have exacerbated matters in the case of the Hurlestons was intermarriage, leading to birth defects and congenital disorders. For example, Anne — one of the four surviving daughters mentioned on the inscription at St. Peter's Church — also married a Geoffrey Shakerley. Sir Geoffrey Shakerley of Civil War fame was his grandfather and Anne's great-grandfather. Anne's mother, Mary, married Roger Barnston as a widow, following John Hurleston's death in 1720, and her younger sister, Elizabeth, married Roger's son, Trafford Barnston. Roger Barnston was therefore Elizabeth Hurleston's step-father and father-in-law. The first Charles Hurleston of Newton Hall had two younger siblings: Elizabeth and William. Respectively, they married William Brock and Elizabeth Brock, brother and sister from nearby Upton Hall. Whilst not all these relationships are consanguineous, they are indicative of marriage within a restricted social circle with potential for negative impact on the gene pool.

Elizabeth Hurleston died in 1735, the year in which her husband too became High Sheriff of Cheshire. The Barnstons were another eminent local family, with estates at Hapsford, Bridge Trafford, and Churton. Trafford Barnston also had a property on the Grosvenor estate in Mayfair and was building a fine town house – Forest House – on Love Street, Chester, at the time of his death in 1771. As he died without issue, despite remarrying after Elizabeth's death, Forest House passed to his nephew, Roger, who also held high civic office and who entertained the Duke of Wellington there in 1817. Trafford's great-grandfather, John, was another ardent Royalist in the Civil War, fighting with the King at Chester and Oxford and being captured and imprisoned for a time in the Tower of London.[35] There is a historic stained-glass window in St. Chad's Church, Farndon, depicting scenes from the Civil War, above the Barnston family crypt.

When the younger Charles Hurleston died childless in 1734, three of his nieces – Anne, Mary, and Elizabeth – survived him. These were the last members of this Hurleston line. His second wife, Susannah, also lived on. She was born at Eccleston in 1704. Her father, Robert, as well as being a servant and friend of the Grosvenor family, was connected to the noble Vernon family of Hodnet. This latter family had been particularly prominent in the court of Elizabeth I.[36] The Hodnet connection explains why it was the location for Charles and Susannah's wedding.

Susannah Hurleston must be the widow referred to in the estate map of 1738 as possessing a jointure in and around Newton Hall. Charles would have made that provision for her for the remainder of her natural life because it was her home. The yellow letters denoting this possession cut through 'Newton Hall and Gardens' but are mostly on fields to the south. The most prominent lettering on the Newton Hall estate and on fields radiating out in all directions is red. A further footnote tells us that 'The Red Letters shew Mad^m Barnstons jointure'. This lady, we assume, was Elizabeth Barnston, née Hurleston. This is not a straightforward deduction, however, as Elizabeth died in 1735 and the map is dated 1738. We can discount the possibility that the lady referred to is Elizabeth's mother — Mary Barnston, following her second marriage — because she had died in 1723. The map, therefore, appears to recognise the dispositions in Charles's will of 1734 but not the fact of Elizabeth's death a year later. A final footnote regarding ownership states, 'The Black Letters shew the land in possession of the Heirs of the Yellow.' These are on fields to the east of the hall, stretching towards Picton, the heirs being Anne and Mary — the two surviving daughters of John Hurleston and nieces of Charles Hurleston — and, by extension, their husbands (see Family Tree D).

Although first to die, Elizabeth was the youngest of Charles's nieces who outlived him, hence the bequest to her being limited to a jointure, full ownership of the property having been conveyed through her eldest sister, Anne. 'Picton,' Hanshall writes in 1817, 'fell to the share of Mary, wife of John Leche, Esq of Carden, in whose descendants it is now vested.'[37] Mary was the second eldest of the surviving nieces. These provisions made elsewhere by Charles explain why neither Anne nor Mary's names appear on the Newton map, despite their ranking ahead of Susannah and Elizabeth in inheritance.

It is also reasonable to assume that the two elder sisters were not lacking in resources before Charles's demise. Although, as mentioned, Anne had married into the wealthy Shakerley family, her husband, Geoffrey

Shakerley, had died at the age of twenty-six in 1733. It appears that the curse of the office of High Sheriff of Cheshire had struck again, as his father — another Sir Geoffrey — occupied this position at the time of his son's death. On 10th January 1738, Anne remarried, this time to John Needham, tenth Viscount Kilmorey, who already owned considerable estates in east Cheshire. This wedding, for reasons seemingly lost in the mists of time, took place in a small parish church in the village of Corsham, Wiltshire.[38] John Needham was painted by Thomas Gainsborough in 1768, probably to celebrate his accession to the title (fig. 11).[39] Newton Hall and surrounding areas were conveyed to the Needham family as a result of this union and parts of the estate remained in their ownership until the 1930s, when they were sold for development.[40] The street names 'Kilmorey Park' and 'Kilmorey Park Avenue' on the western fringes of the township are reminders of the Needham connection to this day. The name 'Kilmorey' relates to land in County Clare, now in the Irish Republic, that was granted to Sir Robert Needham by Charles I in 1625. This was the last Irish peerage to die out, upon the death of Francis Needham in 1961, as re-election was no longer taking place following the creation of the Irish Free State in the 1920s.

The Kilmorey title was elevated to an earldom as a result of the exploits of John and Anne's son, Francis Jack Needham, twelfth Viscount, who was born in 1748. In a distinguished military career, he fought in the American War of Independence — being taken prisoner at Yorktown — and in the French Revolutionary Wars in the 1790s. He became an aide-de-camp to George III in 1793. His best-known victory was as commander of the troops who defeated Irish rebels at the Battle of Arklow in 1798, despite being outnumbered. He lived on to the ripe old age of eighty-four, dying in 1832.[41] His no doubt proud and careworn mother, Anne, had died at one of the Needham family seats, Shavington Hall, in 1786.

Mary Hurleston also married into affluent and noble stock. Her husband, John Leche XIV, was descended from John Leche, who was surgeon, or leech, to Edward III and Richard II in the fourteenth century. Historically, the Hurlestons and the Leches were both renowned hunting families. At the time of the marriage in 1728, the Leche family seat was at Carden Hall (fig. 12), south of Chester, and their town house at 17 Watergate Street in the heart of the city. The hall burnt down in 1912 and the site is now occupied by the Carden Park golf and leisure complex.[42] The Watergate Street property, known as Old Leche House, retains many of its early features, which include a lookout grille, a possible priest hole and decorative allusions to Catherine of Aragon, redolent of Catholic sympathies.

It is interesting to note how the Hurleston name has persisted in the Leche line, even to this day. Mary and John's first daughter was christened Penelope, presumably in memory of Mary's younger sister, who had died at the age of eleven in 1723. Sadly, this Penelope also died young, along with a number of her siblings. William was the only surviving son, being born in 1731. He is a rare example of a male heir in the Leche family not bearing the Christian name 'John'.[43] This was likely to have been the case because John was one of his elder siblings who died in infancy. This supposition is further supported by the fact that William had a son with his wife, Hannah, whom they named 'John Hurleston Leche'. Remarkably, he was sired in 1805 when William would have been seventy-four years old, his wife being almost fifty years his junior. This name continued to be passed down through the generations and there is a John Hurleston Leche alive today. Another family tradition was occupancy of the position of High Sheriff of Cheshire by the head of the family, beginning with William in 1774 and continuing with his son and grandson.

What a fascinating, eventful place Newton Hall must have been in these early days, with powerful, high-born and well-connected people coming and going and momentous family occasions taking place; some sombre, like the passing of Elizabeth Hurleston in 1727; and some joyous, like wedding of Mary Hurleston to John Leche XIV six months later.

Wider developments were taking place within the city of Chester during the fifty years or so in which the Hurleston family occupied Newton Hall. A number of rows — the old public walkways above street-level properties, for which Chester is still renowned today — were enclosed on Lower Bridge Street, following a trend begun by Sir Richard Grosvenor, who moved with his family to their town house, The Falcon, for greater security during the Siege of Chester. In the late 1690s, the Exchange was built in Northgate Street to serve as a common hall, and, in 1712, a life-size statue of Queen Anne was added in a niche on the front elevation. The city walls were repaired and reflagged in the early 1700s. Local politics were dominated by the Grosvenor family, who represented the Tories, but there was often strong and occasionally confrontational opposition from the Whigs. At the 1732 mayoral election, for example, a riot broke out on Bridge Street which necessitated the dragoons being called in to quell it. The Tories once again triumphed.

At a national level, the succession was much disputed, as we have seen. James II visited Chester in 1687, staying at the Bishop's Palace and attending a private Catholic mass at the castle chapel. He was overthrown in the so-called Glorious Revolution the following year and his successor, William III, also visited Chester, in his case in 1690. In 1704, the Duke of Marlborough won an outstanding victory against the French at the Battle of Blenheim, and, in 1707, the Act of Union made Scotland part of Great Britain. Upon Queen Anne's death in 1714, George I and the House of Hanover assumed the monarchy, despite a distant bloodline, in order to maintain the Protestant succession. As we know, the Hurlestons were not always merely interested parties; they were directly involved in or affected by a number of these events.

2

The Property

It is worth taking a moment to consider the architecture of Newton Hall, what its surroundings were like in the Hurlestons' day and how they have been described by historians over the years.

The previous chapter set out circumstantial evidence for the hall having been constructed in the early to mid-1680s. A reading of the architecture of the building bears this out. Most large houses of the period were built of brick, other materials having been legislated against in the aftermath of the Great Fire of London of 1666 and that commodity having become more readily available. Double piled structures were popular; in other words, rectangular blocks that were two rooms deep. There were often two main storeys of similar height, raised above a semi-basement.

The Hurlestons' Caroline allegiances and exile in Holland are highly pertinent here. Followers of Charles II developed a taste for Classical architecture in the Dutch style. At Newton Hall, we see notable features of this style, such as sash windows, a hooded doorway, a plain horizontal string course above the lower windows, a stone cornice above the upper windows, dormer windows set in a steep hipped roof, and square chimneys. A similar style can be seen in the more palatial Belton House in Lincolnshire, which was built between 1685 and 1688, and in aspects of the Binnenhof, the Dutch Parliament building in the Hague.[1] The highlighted quoins at the wall angles and the balustered parapet on the roof are more closely associated with the Queen Anne period than the late seventeenth century, which may have led to misattribution by some observers. However, features such as this were not new but were simply coming back into vogue, and the Hurlestons may have been at the forefront of that trend. Analogous surviving properties include Uppark House in Sussex (quoins) and Dyrham Park in Gloucestershire (parapet), both of which were commissioned circa 1690. The Building Act of 1707 outlawed projecting wooden eaves, requiring brick parapets instead. It is possible that the parapet at Newton Hall was added in response to this legislation.

Beyond the architecture, other original features of the property survived until the most recent conversion in the 1990s. These include a powder closet covered by wood panelling in one of the rooms and a dovecote and well to the rear of the hall. The well, which was filled in for safety, and the presence of a water source in the area may have been one of the attractions of the location for the Hurlestons, who had other land at their disposal. The fact that Well Lane lies a short distance from Newton Hall adds weight to this supposition. The dovecote is proof of the estate's manorial origins. Dovecotes date back to the

Norman Conquest and the right to keep them was the exclusive privilege of the aristocratic elite up to the seventeenth century. Until the mid-1940s there was a servants' staircase leading from the large basement kitchen to the top storey, where the floors sloped markedly for the greater ease of cleaning.[2]

In terms of the surroundings, the 1738 estate map shows the hall and a number of nearby buildings, mostly rectangular in shape. At least three of these were longer than the hall itself. They are presumed to be a mixture of workers' cottages, stables and other outbuildings. The lack of defined roadways around these properties, coupled with the fact that they are all on land owned by the Hurlestons or their inheritors, indicates that they were integral to the estate. The gardens, which appear to contain neat rows of trees or shrubbery, extend for a distance to the north and, to a lesser extent, to the south of the hall. There is a road following the line of the modern-day Newton Hall Drive which continues northwards and stops at the end of the gardens. At right angles to this is another road leading from the entrance of the hall across to what we now know as Kingsway (apparently named after a route believed to have been followed by Charles I). There is little development to the north of the estate, but to the south, the lines of Wealstone Lane, Well Lane, Brook Lane and Newton Lane can be clearly made out.

As already mentioned, directories — most notably the *Post Office Directory* of 1878 and *Kelly's Directory* of 1923 — make confident assertions about extensive and well-wooded grounds and the fact that the property was originally moated. Whilst the arboreal character of the grounds is beyond dispute — as fine, mature trees in the area today affirm — the existence of a moat is more difficult to prove. There is no sign of it on the 1738 map, or where the line of it may have run. Nor do the design of the house or the multiple access routes around it suggest it was built with defensive features in mind. Additionally, moats had outlived their usefulness beyond Tudor times as they provided no protection against siege artillery of the type used so forcefully against the city of Chester in the Civil War. That said, country houses often had moats simply as a feature in their own right or as a symbol of the status of the owner. There is a moat at Upton Grange, approximately half a mile to the north, which may well at one time have been on Hurleston land. The fashion dates from medieval times, well before Newton Hall came into being.[3] A possible scenario, therefore, is that there was a moat around a property which previously stood on the Newton Hall site, but not around the hall itself. A more likely feature was a ha-ha, if not two. There are slight downhill inclines moving away from the hall and parallel to it for a distance at the northern and southern extremities of the playing fields at Chester University's Kingsway campus. As this land was originally on the Newton Hall estate, the ha-ha theory may well hold good.

Historians who have commented on Newton Hall have not been reticent in offering an opinion of its aesthetic appeal, or lack of it. George Ormerod, an eminent figure in the field and a prime source of information, described the hall in his epic work *History of the County Palatine and City of Chester* (1816–1819) as 'the residence of the later generations of the Hurlestons, a brick building with a high Dutch roof, the situation flat and uninteresting'.[4] A contemporary, J. H. Hanshall, writing a year or two later, said of the building that 'it is of brick with a high roof and scarcely any feature to recommend it in point of situation'.[5] It is almost certain that Ormerod, who liked to gather information first-hand where possible, viewed the property. It is also reasonable to assume that Hanshall did not and that he simply read and reformulated Ormerod's report and opinion.

Whatever the fact of the matter, the judgements seem harsh. There are accounts elsewhere of the hall having views of Beeston Castle and the sandstone ridge to the south. This is still true today, although the view is slightly obscured by now mature trees in the foreground. There are also fine views of the city of Chester and beyond — with the cathedral prominent on the skyline, and the Welsh hills to the west — as there would have been when the hall was built and later when Ormerod was writing about it. It seems fair to suppose that he was not invited in and was therefore unable to appreciate the prospect from the upper floors.

Ormerod's tendency towards pejorative judgements is further reflected in what he says about the Hurlestons' other erstwhile domain of Picton, as reported by Hanshall:

> Mr Ormerod with great propriety says, in his description of this township that 'in roads, appearance and inhabitants it may safely be said to present a complete picture of barbarism'.[6]

These are uncompromising words from Ormerod, suggesting that perhaps the situation of Newton Hall was not so bad after all. This passage is also further evidence of

Hanshall's reliance on Ormerod and his deference towards him.

Set against Ormerod and Hanshall's opinion of the location is a seventeenth-century observation from a traveller who describes 'beholding on our left Newton, the lordship of John Hurlestone, Esq, which was once one of those sweet morsels that the Abbot and his Convent kept for their own wholesome provision'.[7]

The situation and the presence of a water source may have been part of the appeal for the Hurlestons when selecting a site for Newton Hall, but there would have been other influential factors too. They owned the land and perhaps wanted to position the main family seat nearer the city, where they were known to have business and relationships, and where the last Charles Hurleston was resident for a while. A good illustration of their life and associates in the area is provided by Roger Whitley in a diary extract of 30th November 1686:

> I went to Chester with Mainwaring in the coach to meete the Bishop; the rest went on horseback; we met the Bishop at Flooke Brooke; brought him to the Palace; stayd ½ houer with him; went back to Flooke Brook; there was Hurleston, his sonne, Griffith, Minshall, Mainwaring, my sonne, Swetnam, Morgan &c. dined there, parted about 5; went to the Sunne; there we found G.Mainwaring, Edwards, Lloyd, Murrey, Golborne, Ravenscroft; we parted at 10.

'Flooke Brooke' would have been Flookersbrook Hall, rebuilt by this time following its destruction in the Civil

War. The bishop was Thomas Cartwright and the palace is the property in which James II would stay the following year. Although an Anglican bishop, Cartwright was close to the King, having been chaplain to him and his brothers in their youth. This loyalty remained through his monarchy and deposition. Cartwright followed James into exile in France and Ireland, where he was to die.

The Hurlestons referred to by Whitley would have been fifty-eight-year-old John and his twenty-eight-year-old son, Charles. It is impossible to know what the purpose of the gathering at Flookersbrook was or what the relationships may have been between those whom Whitley mentions. However, if they were united in their support for the Stuart line, it is interesting to follow that thread through to the next Charles Hurleston — grandson and nephew of John and Charles respectively — and his deliberations over the regal claims of James's son at Ashley Hall almost thirty years later. There would also have been a painful irony in the fact that, in 1688, the elder Charles Hurleston — by this time head of the family — was one of a number of Cheshire men required by Parliament to help fund the invasion by William and Mary through extraordinary taxation.[8]

Newton Hall was awarded Grade II* listed status on 8th May 1950. The asterisk is a significant mark of added protection as approximately 92% of protected buildings carry Grade II status, according to Historic England. At this level, Newton Hall is on a par with Liverpool Metropolitan Cathedral and Battersea Power Station. It outranks, for example, Abbey Road Studios and the BT

Tower in London.

The last survey of Newton Hall by Historic England took place in 1992. It describes the building as a 'Small country house. c1700. Stone-dressed brick with hipped grey slate roof ... chimneys with arched panels in late C17 manner'. This is a further indication that the hall pre-dates the reign of Queen Anne.

A relatively recent reference to Newton Hall can be found in the 2011 publication *The Buildings of England: Cheshire*, as follows:

> Newton Hall survives amongst suburban housing off Park Drive. Square block of c1700 raised up on a semi-basement with hipped roof that looks as though it should have a cupola, behind a balustraded parapet and heavy cornice. Sash windows at front but casement remaining at side.[9]

The reference to Park Drive is confusing as it is at least half a mile away on the other side of Hoole Road. The architectural detail is valid, however. There is no evidence of a cupola ever having been in situ on the building.

The interior is now necessarily quite different from the way it was pre-conversion and only a few of the original features survive to this day. These include exposed oak beams, which add an old-world aesthetic to a number of the flats, and the broad and ample staircase which dominates the centre of the building. Wide staircases were deemed important by those who were able to afford them, partly for their bright and capacious feel in daylight and partly to allow people to pass each other in the darkness, before the advent of gas lighting. It is said that the property contains the largest single-piece oak banister in the country. One or two flats retain what appear to be wrought-iron Victorian era fireplaces. Modern forms of heating have undermined their purpose but they remain attractive features from another bygone age.

3

The Late Eighteenth and Early Nineteenth Century

Records relating to occupancy at Newton Hall in the wake of Charles Hurleston's death in 1734 become somewhat sparse. Perhaps that is understandable in the circumstances. As mentioned, his niece, Elizabeth, died the following year and her sisters and co-heiresses, Mary and Anne, had married and moved into their new homes. Charles's widow, Susannah, would have continued living in her jointure at Newton Hall and would have retained staff to attend to her needs and maintain the estate. Although we know she was born in 1704, her date of death is uncertain. It is possible that she enjoyed some longevity and stayed at the property well into the eighteenth century.

In any event, ownership continued to be vested in the Kilmoreys, who subsequently let it out. In August 1775, we find a Henry Hesketh of the Manor of Newton named in a 'Deed to lead to the uses of a recovery', which relates to the requirement to transfer property pursuant to a fine from a subordinate to a superior tenant.[1] No details of the property in question or the circumstances around the case are known but it fixes Henry at Newton, and in all probability at the manor house of Newton Hall, at this time. Once again, we have an instance of a father and son bearing the same name. Henry, the father, was born in Bowdon, south of Manchester, in 1724 but was active in Chester from a young age, including siring a daughter who was baptised at Holy Trinity in the city in 1742, sadly dying two years later. His son, Henry, is also reported to have been born in Chester, in his case in 1751 (see Family Tree E). Records show the first of these Henrys to have been Sheriff of Chester in 1749-1750 and Mayor in 1762-1763, so he was clearly well-established in the city at that time. His name is also inscribed on the Bridge Gate (fig. 13) as one of two murengers responsible for raising funds for its construction in 1782, six years before his death.

The Heskeths were wine merchants, related to a Liverpool branch of the family who owned vineyards in Portugal through their interests in the company *Offley, Campion, Hesketh Co*. Records from the Port of Chester show them as regular importers of wine and spirits at this time.[2] The trade between Great Britain and Portugal, concentrated around the Douro River and Oporto, flourished in the eighteenth and early nineteenth century. The Heskeths shared in this success, as contemporary descriptions of their assets show. Hemingway, writing in 1831, describes their business premises, located in a building which still exists at the junction of Watergate Street and Trinity Street in Chester, as 'an excellent brick building, faced with stone, now the property of Henry

Hesketh esq and occupied by his son, Henry Hesketh Jr. esq' (fig. 14).[3]

By this time there was a further generation of the family, including another Henry who is the 'Jr.' mentioned here. Hemingway goes on to give us a further insight into the grandfather's wealth and lifestyle in the following reference to the building we know today as Stanley Palace:

> This decayed mansion is a striking example of the mutability of all human affairs. I believe it is the former city residence of the Derby family, on account of its contiguity to the Watergate, of which the Earl of Derby had the custody. It is now the joint property of Mr Boden and Mr E Hodgkinson, builders. About the middle of the last century, it was occupied by the father of Henry Hesketh esq and, I am credibly informed that during the races, was a place of general resort for the carriages of gentlemen attending Chester during those festivities.

He is correct in making the connection between the property and the Earls of Derby, whose family name was Stanley. Perhaps we have reason to be thankful to Messrs Boden and Hodgkinson for preserving this fine Tudor edifice into modern times.

The commercial success of the wine enterprise may not have been a constant, however. Henry Hesketh is listed as a bankrupt as at 23rd April 1793 — the year in which Henry Jr. was born — in a document published by William Smith and Co of Lombard St, London.[4] That was not marked as 'final', however, and there is a note to say it was superseded in June of the same year, so it appears the business survived and, in due course, prospered once again.

There were four daughters too, born between 1785 and 1795 at Newton. The most notable of these was the youngest, Emma Anne Hesketh. She appears to have been very public-spirited from an early age, founding and equipping the *Flookersbrook, Hoole and Newton Female Friendly Society*. Her mother, Jane, was president and benefactor and her sisters were involved too. *The Chester Courant* reported on the first annual event at Whitsuntide in 1816, which appeared to be quite a grand affair, beginning and ending with a fete at The Ermine public house, punctuated by a procession to and service at Chester Cathedral. By all accounts, these events continued up to the early 1840s.

The source from which this material is extracted states that 'the prime organisers were the Hesketh family who lived at Newton Hall'.[5] Although a trusted source, we need to be circumspect with this information. The 1792 *Commercial Directory of Chester* describes Newton as 'the seat of Henry Hesketh' in much the same way as it was described as the 'seat of the Hurlestons' in earlier times. It is therefore a reasonable assumption that they were tenants of Viscount Kilmorey at Newton Hall. At some point in this period, they appear to have bought and built upon part of the estate. Writing in 1817, Ormerod, having given his unadulterated view on the location of Newton Hall, adds: 'Another house in this township is the property of the heirs or assignes of Henry Hesketh esq.' Hanshall follows up soon afterwards by describing it as 'a handsome mansion'. We can see from a tithe map of circa 1840 that the Heskeths had acquired land adjacent to Newton Hall, which would have formed part of the jointures of both Madam Hurleston and Madam Barnston, as detailed in the

1738 map. As these ladies were both long deceased, the land would have been pooled amongst the substantial estates of the Kilmorey family, who were unlikely to have had a strong ongoing practical interest in using or maintaining it. If the Heskeths had the wherewithal to buy and build upon the land, it is no surprise that such a transaction was possible.

It is not clear which of the Henrys completed the purchase and built the property, known as Newton House (fig. 15), but it is most likely to have been the second as the architecture of the building aligned most directly with his lifespan. It bore characteristics of the Regency period, which began in the 1790s, reinforcing the hypothesis that the Heskeths lived at Newton Hall before this time. These included stucco walls — popularised by the great Regency architect, John Nash — and a generous, low-pitched slate roof, becoming increasingly common around the turn of the eighteenth century due to the greater availability of Welsh slate.

The Newton House estate comprised approximately forty acres and was located immediately to the north of Newton Hall, on the other side of what is now Plas Newton Lane. This was split across ten plots with one of the largest being occupied by the house, gardens and lawn and another containing cottages and gardens. This was an estate to rival Newton Hall itself, though we now know it did not enjoy the same longevity. The original Newton House was demolished in the early 1990s and replaced by the care home — also named Newton House — which stands on the site today. The tied cottages remain as a short terrace of privately owned homes at the junction of Bank Close and Plas Newton Lane, and some walls from the old estate can still be seen around the perimeter of the modern-day Newton House.[6]

The Newton Hall estate seems to have diminished in other ways in the century or so between the two maps (fig. 16). The buildings to the east and west have disappeared and the well-laid-out paths and wooded areas no longer feature. Curiously, the road across the front of the hall has gone too, along with the road that runs at right angles to it. The access now appears to be from Newton Lane, which had not existed on the 1738 map. This may explain why there are two buildings today which style themselves 'Newton Hall Lodge' — one on Plas Newton Lane and one on Newton Hall Drive — as there may have been more than one lodge serving the property over time. The Plas Newton country house and estate, of which we will hear more, had just come into being by 1840 and this probably explains developments in the road network. The Hesketh estate was accessed by a spur off Newton Lane — just to the north of the junction with Wealstone Lane — which followed the same path that it does today, apart from the fact that it looped behind the grassy area at the top of what we now know as Queensway in the same semi-circular course.

Can we infer from this that Newton Hall had experienced a period of decline and degeneration up to this point? It is certainly true that the grounds had reduced in size and most outbuildings had gone, but it remained occupied and, from what we can gather, by people who could afford to be discriminating about where they lived. Soon we will turn to the Parker family, who feature at the hall from the early nineteenth century onwards, but first we must close out on the fortunes — good and ill — of the Heskeths.

After the financial difficulties of the early 1790s, the family business enjoyed a period of stability, which lasted for the next two decades or so. The old commercial directories of Chester tell us that Henry Hesketh Sr. was at the helm in 1815, when he was approaching his mid-sixties, but that by 1822 his son had assumed control.[7]

Amongst their clients were the renowned 'Ladies of Llangollen', Sarah Ponsonby and Eleanor Butler. These lifelong partners and doyens of contemporary literary society had settled in Llangollen — approximately 25 miles south-west of Chester — in 1780, having slipped the social shackles of their native Ireland to pursue their unconventional lifestyle in this quiet corner of north Wales. A panoply of eminent visitors to their home included the poets Shelley, Byron and Wordsworth and the writer, Sir Walter Scott. A letter from these ladies to 'Henry Hesketh Esq, Newton near Chester', dated 1st September 1817, conveys their profuse apologies for a long delay in settling their account, which they ascribe to the 'tediousness of Irish remittances', occasioning them the 'greatest uneasiness'. They also take the opportunity in this correspondence to pass on their best regards to the Hesketh family — 'especially our friend Miss Mary Hesketh' — and place a further order for two or three dozen of the 'best and most fashionable white wines', in anticipation of 'some visitors whom we are extremely anxious to entertain well'. The identity of these particular visitors is unknown.

A subsequent letter from the ladies, on 7th July 1818, strikes a different tone. This time it is addressed to 'Mr. Huxley at the Wine Vaults of H. Hesketh Esq, Chester'. It complains of 'having tried four successive bottles of the last Bucellas' and being 'greatly distressed at their having been every one found sour and unfit for drinking'. It also requests a dozen more bottles of guaranteed good quality, offering to return the few remaining bottles from the previous consignment.[8] There is no continuation in the correspondence in the source material and no insight at all into the Hesketh side of it. Perhaps it is telling that Henry is no longer managing the relationship directly, despite the distinguished palates for which his merchandise is destined.

Moving on, we are fortunate to have a vivid account of the census-taking process in Newton in 1821, in which the Heskeths are mentioned in the passing.[9] It also gives us an insight into some of the challenges faced by the enumerator at a time when the process was in its infancy. In this extract we see Henry asserting his right to privacy:

> Henry Hesketh had a remarkable household about him, who would neither supply the census taker with names nor ages and it is thus described: 'One male between 60 and 70; one male between 30 and 40; one male between 20 and 30; one female between 50 and 60; and three females between 30 and 40'.

The two Henrys were seventy and twenty-eight years old respectively. Mrs Jane Hesketh was fifty-six, the three elder daughters were in their thirties, and Emma was twenty-six. It is therefore possible that most of the family members were recorded, although, of course, staff and visitors may also be included in the count. Two of the daughters — Frances and Emma — had married by this time and were likely to have been elsewhere.

It is a pity the household was not more receptive to the census-taker because he has been unsparing in the detail he provides of encounters with others in the neighbourhood. Age, it seems, was a delicate and imprecise subject. We are told that 'Margaret Dodd was honest enough to avow her years at 59 ... but three other females who lived with her could neither be frightened nor coaxed to give their ages and they are accordingly bracketed as being between 40 and 50'. Reading on, we are made aware that:

> William and Elizabeth Deakin had a family of five children, four lads and a girl, but 'they'd be hanged if they know'd the ages of the older ones', and three of them are accordingly returned as being between 5 and 10, one as 4 and the wench, 'god bless her sweet 'art' as 1 year old. But their names we cannot have because 'what cou'd it matter'n to the King as to how they was cau'd'.

None of this anecdotal information can be corroborated because the 1821 census was not broken down on an individual basis. We would need to wait until 1841 for that level of detail. Regrettably, there was also no reference to Newton Hall. It is possible that the census-taker simply did not come upon it — even today it can prove elusive to visitors because of its sequestered location.

The marriages of this generation of the Hesketh family — insofar as they took place at all, as Elizabeth and Mary appear to have remained single — were notable (see Family Tree F). They have this in common with the last generation of the Hurlestons.

Frances was first to wed, in 1810. Her husband was Richard William Howard Vyse, who was descended from a bishop of Lichfield through his father's line and Thomas Wentworth, first Earl of Strafford, through his mother's. The Vyse family still held senior clerical offices at Lichfield at this time. Thomas Wentworth was Lord Deputy of Ireland under Charles I and was executed for conspiring against the Long Parliament in 1641. Despite this notoriety, the family retained considerable estates in Northamptonshire, which devolved to Richard Vyse almost two centuries later. At the time of his marriage to Frances, he was MP for Beverley, later exchanging this for Honiton in Devon. His main career was in the military, where he achieved the rank of major-general in 1846. Concurrent with this, he took an active interest in Egyptology and was involved in excavations at the Pyramids of Giza, publishing seminal works on the topic. Richard and Frances had eight sons and two daughters together.[10] Frances died in 1841 and so did not live to see her husband's most notable successes. Richard himself died twelve years later.

The next of the Hesketh siblings to marry was Emma, in 1819. Her husband was the Reverend Thomas Blackburne, minister of the parish church of Eccles and son of John Ireland Blackburne, MP for Warrington. In this capacity she continued her charitable and public-spirited work, teaching Sunday school for the children of local mill workers and keeping a store of medicinal remedies for use by the poor. Her defining moment, however, came when she was caught up in the historic events of 15th September 1830, when the world's first passenger railway was opened, and Stephenson's *Rocket* travelled between

Liverpool and Manchester. Early in the day, in the absence of her husband, she alerted fifty special constables to the need to guard Eccles Bridge against potential unrest at the arrival of the Duke of Wellington, who, as prime minister at that time, was unpopular for resisting reform. Later came the tragic death of William Huskisson, MP for Liverpool, following an accident involving *Rocket* on the track nearby. He was taken in his mortally wounded state to the vicarage, where Emma nursed him until he passed away that night. Her 'activity, sense and conduct' were commended in *The Manchester Courier* and *The Times* and remembered with gratitude by Huskisson's widow, Emily.[11]

Emma and the Reverend Thomas had twelve children. He died suddenly in 1847 and she lived out the remainder of her life between her new home at Spring Hill, Boughton, Chester, and Crewe Hall, as she was related to the Crewe family, who owned that splendid property. Two of her sons, Henry and Foster Grey, followed their father into the ministry, the former becoming an honorary canon at Chester Cathedral. Emma died at Spring Hill at the age of ninety in 1886, and a stained-glass window was installed at the cathedral to commemorate her life.

In 1823, Emma's brother Henry married Margaret Hilton, daughter of James Hilton, silk merchant, of Pennington Hall near Leigh. This was about the time that this Henry was assuming control of the Hesketh family business in Chester. The boom years in the Portuguese wine trade of the previous century – engendered by favourable trading arrangements, British domination of the seas and general prosperity – had waned. Blockades of ports on the Iberian peninsula as part of Napoleon's naval campaigns, a Portuguese civil war between 1828 and 1834 and a succession of bad harvests along the Douro River had further drastic effects on supply. Economic hardship in Britain undermined the demand for port, which was seen as a luxury item.[12] The aggregation of these pressures amounted to a significant threat to the business.

It was no surprise therefore to see the Heskeths being petitioned for bankruptcy again in the 1830s. The petition was raised in 1833 against a William Thomas and Henry Hesketh Sr., who was still alive in that year. It was then deferred until 1838, by which time both respondents had died.[13] The lack of involvement of Henry Jr. points to the conclusion that the business had already been wound down and that he had disengaged from it. There is evidence to suggest that this situation placed the family under some financial strain, despite inherited wealth and connections. In 1836, Henry Sr. had advertised two plots of land in for sale in Upton — Mill Field and The Knowle. In the event, these did not sell, as they appear in his son's ownership in the map of 1840, so the bankruptcy petition must have been dealt with through other means.

Beyond this point, Henry Jr. appears to have relocated to the north Wales coast and reinvented himself. The 1847 'Tourist Guide of Wales' makes reference to the 'increasing and respectable village of Colwyn' and tells us that 'Glan-y-Don, the seat of H. Hesketh esq, is in this neighbourhood'. Traces of the building that he lived in have been lost as a later 'Glan-y-Don Hall' was erected on the site in 1910, becoming Colwyn Bay Civic Centre in 1964. Most recently, it was sold in 2019 for private development and conversion into apartments.[14] The location and later history suggest it was a sizeable and attractive place for Henry to live and the mention of him in particular in the tourist guide implies that he had retained some social prominence and financial heft. This is confirmed in the 1851 census, in which he is shown at this address as a 'gentleman', living with his wife and seven servants.

Henry was to die two years later at the age of sixty. An entry in the Liverpool Mercury of 11th October 1853 tells us that 'Edward Swetenham esq of the North Wales and Chester Circuit has been appointed the distributor of stamps for the Chester District, void by the decease of the late Henry Hesketh esq'. The office of distributor of stamps was a responsible one. Holders were appointed by the Board of Commissioners for Stamps and there were ninety-five of them throughout Great Britain in 1821.[15] The most famous incumbent was the poet William Wordsworth, who occupied the post in the county of Westmorland from 1813 to 1843. The positions were well-paid and mostly supported by able and active deputies. This may have allowed Henry some semblance of retirement later in life, even though he appears to have died in post and unexpectedly.

Returning to the Newton Hall of Henry's youth, we also encounter the Parker family (see Family Tree G). There is a tablet in Lichfield Cathedral which bears the following inscription:

> A grateful family dedicate this stone with filial reverence to the memory of their Mother, Elizabeth, Daughter of John Turton of Orgreave, in this county

Esquire, and the wife of George Parker of Newton Hall in the County of Chester, Esquire. She died on 3rd of June, 1808 in the 62nd year of her age.[16]

The location and reporting of this inscription suggest that there was some pedigree in the family, and that indeed proves to be the case. It also places George Parker clearly and unequivocally at Newton Hall at this time. Two years later, we are told that Newton Hall 'is owned by Viscount Kilmorey but rented to George Parker' in a publication entitled *The Landed Gentry and Aristocracy in 1810*.

Elizabeth Parker, née Turton, was from a well-heeled family. A survey for hearth tax conducted in the Orgreave area in 1666 assessed eighty properties and found the manor house of John Turton — from whom Elizabeth was directly descended — to be the largest with eleven hearths. Orgreave is a few miles north of Lichfield, in the parish of Alrewas. Soon after the survey was taken, the Turton family moved to the newly-built Orgreave Hall, a fine country residence which still exists as a private home today. This is where Elizabeth would have been born. In 1752, the Turtons sold the manor of Alrewas to the Anson family, who were later Earls of Lichfield.[17]

The Parkers were originally from Derbyshire but settled in Staffordshire in the early eighteenth century. One of George's ancestors from this period — also called George Parker — was a prosperous yeoman who bought and built upon the Park Hall estate at Caverswall, south of Lichfield. The family suffered the same fate as the Hurlestons in the Civil War when George's son, William, who came out for the King, had his estates confiscated and, in his case, not returned until after the Restoration. He was also imprisoned for a spell in Stafford Gaol.[18]

Thomas Parker, the father of George Parker who lived at Newton Hall in the early nineteenth century, achieved high office, becoming Lord Chief Baron of the Exchequer, a post he held for thirty years. He was knighted for his services. He married twice, having two sons from his first marriage and two daughters from his second. His eldest son was another Sir Thomas, who became High Sheriff of Staffordshire. His youngest daughter married Sir John Jervis, Admiral of the Fleet, who was also first Earl of St. Vincent and a major figure in the American War of Independence and Napoleonic Wars. The wider Parker family in the eighteenth century included a Lord Chief Justice and a President of the Royal Society.

George occupied Park Hall in his early adulthood and no doubt met and married Elizabeth Turton as a result of family connections in the Lichfield area. George was still in situ at Park Hall in 1791 when the building caught fire after a long dry spell and was damaged beyond repair. He stayed in the area to oversee the rebuilding of the property, moving to Newton Hall sometime after that.[19] His motivation for relocating to Chester is not certain but we do know that he had strong connections with the city through his offspring.

In total, George and Elizabeth appear to have had nine children — five sons and four daughters (see Family Tree H). We see once again that the female line was more resilient than the male, as all the daughters but only one of the sons survived into middle-age or beyond. When George himself died in 1819, four of his sons — George, John, Thomas, and Edward — had predeceased him. Notable amongst these was Edward, the youngest son, who died in 1814 fighting for the Duke of Wellington against Napoleon's forces at the Battle of Orthez in Portugal, towards the end of the Peninsula War. George was survived by his third son, William, and his daughters Martha, Ann, Elizabeth and Frances.

George's will (fig. 17) – drafted at and rooted in Newton Hall – is worth examining. It is held at the National Archives and written in an elaborate and barely legible hand. The effort of obtaining and deconstructing it, however, is rewarded with some telling insights into family relationships and bonds, domestic life at Newton Hall in the early nineteenth century, and glimpses into the character and mindset of the man himself.

It is determined that the funeral should take place at St. Oswald's, which was the south transept of Chester Cathedral and the focal point of the parish in which Newton still resided at the time. He then proceeds to describe the type of coffin and ceremony he would like and to stipulate who the pallbearers should be and how they should be attired and remunerated. His appetite is for a simple, respectful occasion. Turning to his family, he reflects, 'My son – alas, only one – is better provided for than his sisters ... Martha, Ann and Frances.' He then commends those three unmarried daughters for their 'dutiful and amiable conduct towards their beloved and most constant mother and myself' and leaves them all the furniture, plate, silver, china and books of their choice in or at Newton Hall. He also leaves them his stock of cows and pigs and, somewhat less charitably, requests that 'the old mare be shot'.

The impression this creates is of a son who is removed from the business of the hall but of three daughters who are intimately involved in it. They are left items which doubtless are of considerable intrinsic worth but they are also of day-to-day practical value. The livestock would have been a means of sustenance and occupation in what would still have been a largely agricultural environment outside the confines of the city, and Newton Hall has all the trappings of a working farm.

The reason for the exclusion of George's other daughter, Elizabeth, from the earlier provisions of his will becomes clearer in his next stipulation:

> If my dearest daughter Nuttall will accept of my miniature picture I should wish it as a token that would remind her of an affectionate father who would have done more if poor dear John had not provided so handsomely for her.

She was widow to a man called John Nuttall, who had taken care of her financially. It can be supposed from the offer of the picture that she lived away from Newton Hall, where it was probably on display at the time of the drafting of the will. Towards the end of the document, there is mention of the children from this union — another John, and Emma — who would have been fifteen and five years old, respectively, when their grandfather died. The first child of his surviving son, William, was not born until five years later, so these were George's only grandchildren at the time.

Referring to the grandson, the will states: 'My watch with a new pinch back chain and the watch new gilt I give to dear John Nuttall — it may perhaps serve him till his ability present him a gold one.' It then goes on to prescribe his funeral attire in the following terms: 'To said John I request a strong fustian suit of Jarret and Browns instead of mourning with any striped waistcoat of flannel.' It is easy to infer from this an impression of John as a teenager with unfulfilled potential and an eye for the latest fashions. The reference to 'Browns' may well be connected to the famous department store, *Browns of Chester*, which was originally established on Eastgate Street by Susannah Brown in 1791.

The words used in relation to Emma are touching and sincere: 'To dearest little Emma I trust ten guineas may be given as a small token of my love and remembrance due to so amiable and promising a child.' The monetary amount is difficult to evaluate in modern-day terms, but it is probably approaching £1,000. It can also be assessed against other bequests in the will. Servants Mary Burton, Hannah Burton and Eleanor Taylor are to have five guineas added to their wages for their 'faithful' and 'excellent' service. Elizabeth Bentley and James Roberts are awarded a three-guinea bonus each for their 'steady conduct'. Mary Burton is also given shirts, handkerchiefs and white linen, not just to launder but to keep. This recognition, albeit stratified, is likely to have promoted loyalty as there was clearly an appetite to keep the household together after George's death.

Additionally, the will contains such exhortations as: 'The manuscripts in my revered father's stamp and the books in the dark closet should not be parted with out of respect to the venerable author.' There are also two references to the need for the family to support an ailing 'Patty', whose fuller identity and condition are unknown. George Parker died on 25th January 1819 at the age of eighty-four and the will was proved on 23rd August that year.

It is worth considering the Nuttall family in more detail, not least because of the way their story intersects with the story of Newton Hall in the first half of the nineteenth century. The manner in which George addresses Elizabeth as 'daughter Nuttall' in his will is striking — especially given her widowed status — and in stark contrast with her sisters, whose Christian names are used. To some extent, this reflects the mores of the time, when a married woman's status and identity were inextricably bound up with her husband's, whether he was alive or not. In Elizabeth's case this is likely to have been accentuated by the financial hold he exercised over her from beyond the grave.

John Nuttall Sr. was undoubtedly a wealthy man. He came from a family who owned substantial lands in Lancashire and who were involved in lucrative trade with the Dutch. He may well have been a descendent of the John Nuttall who was granted land by Queen Elizabeth I at the same time as Richard Hurleston, as mentioned in Chapter 1. His father Robert founded and liberally endowed Bury Grammar School. John himself was born in 1776 and is described a 'gentleman commoner of Balliol College, Oxford'.[20] Despite his studies, he married at the age of sixteen, but not to Elizabeth at this point. His bride was Eliza Howard and the ceremony took place at Manchester Cathedral. She died in 1799, a year after giving birth to a son, Robert. Five years later John sired another son, John Jr. — this time with Elizabeth Parker.

The birth took place in Bury but before long they would be living in Cheshire, first at Norley Bank, approximately twelve miles east of Chester, then at Overleigh Hall in Chester itself. Overleigh was a grand property in extensive grounds, built soon after the Restoration by Thomas Cowper, whose town house still stands in Bridge Street, Chester. The Cowpers were a high-profile local family, many of whom occupied important civic posts in the city in the eighteenth and nineteenth century. Like the Hurlestons and their associates, the Cowpers were ardent Royalists in the Civil War, which makes it all the more surprising that they kept a valuable collection of portraits of Oliver Cromwell and his family at Overleigh — or perhaps explains it. The estate was inherited by Charles Cholmondeley of Vale Royal through marriage in 1788 and let back to Harriet Cowper for a life term which ended with her death in 1811. The Nuttall family's ensuing tenancy there was short-lived, as John died in November 1813, when Emma was a baby. A letter dated 16th March 1814 from Mrs. E. Nuttall of Overleigh Hall to a Mrs. Whitaker of Simonstone, near Burnley, survives in the Lancashire Archives. It explains that Mrs. Nuttall had at last been able to release her cook for Mrs. Whitaker's service, presumably preparatory to vacating the premises. Overleigh Hall then became a school for a few years before the estate was acquired in 1821 by Robert, second Earl Grosvenor, and demolished for the construction of the driveway to Eaton Hall in 1830.[21]

The relationship between George Parker and John Nuttall was evidently a close one. The words 'poor dear John' in George's will have overtones of lamentation more than five years after John's death. The contents of John's own will provide further clues as to the strength of the relationship. What is immediately noticeable in comparing the two wills is the fact that the handwriting is almost identical. This raises the prospect of them having been set down by the same scribe, who, in the case of John's will, writes more clearly as a younger man, perhaps with a steadier hand and more assiduous in his duties. This document is dated 9th October 1813 — the month before John died — and George Parker's daughter, Ann, is one of the witnesses. George's daughter, Elizabeth, is indeed liberally endowed with hundreds of pounds per annum in rents and annuities, along with valuable goods and chattels, including horses, carriages, furniture, china, plate, and wines, spirits and liquors. These latter items could well have been supplied by Henry Hesketh, in part at least. The strict proviso, oft repeated in the will, is that these bequests would become 'revoked and void' if Elizabeth remarried.

The three children — Robert from his first marriage and John and Emma from his second — are all provided for too. Lump sums of several thousand pounds each are set aside, apportioned in favour of the sons, and Robert in particular as the eldest. Emma's bequest is £5,000. These amounts are all due at the age of twenty-one and to be held in trust in the meantime, all three being minors at the time of John's death. One of the trustees is 'George Parker of London', suggesting that he had business there and re-affirming the close relationship that must have existed between John and George. There is a sufficient spread of trustees to mitigate against the death of one or more of them during the period of trusteeship. If Elizabeth were to forfeit her inheritance by remarrying, her assets would be pooled in the same trust. This potentially creates a position, perhaps unintended, where George would be a trustee of the fortune of which his daughter has been deprived.

George's will is a strong indication that he expected his three unmarried daughters — Martha, Ann and Frances, in age order — to continue to live at Newton Hall after his death, supported by their legacies. This appears not to have been borne out by reality as there is a record of a Martha Parker being buried at St. Oswald's at about the same time as him. This is not conclusively the Martha Parker of Newton Hall but there is no trace of her being alive after that in publicly available sources.

Another pertinent question is the extent of William Parker's involvement with Newton Hall. This must necessarily have been limited on account of the nature of his career and, like a number of his forebears, his distinguished professional life. In his case, this began at the tender age of twelve, when he entered the navy. A beautifully written letter survives which he penned on 24th February 1793 from on board the ship *Orion,* which was docked in Southampton before what was to be his first voyage.[22] It is clear that his great-uncle, John Jervis, then a vice-admiral, had ensured that William would be well cared for by the ship's command, as the positive tone and content of the letter confirms. After William has spoken in very mature fashion about naval affairs, there is a stark reminder of his youth in the words, 'My father has furnished me with a box of colours, drawing books and everything that could possibly amuse me'. Revealingly for us, there is mention elsewhere in the letter of 'Patty', whom William wants to be reassured that he does not sleep in a hammock but in a cot, 'which is a much more comfortable thing'. Perhaps Patty, who shows such concern for his welfare, occupied the role of a nanny or governess in the Parker household. She was certainly integral to it, as George Parker's will — written at Newton Hall twenty-six years later — avers.

After that, William's rise through the ranks was mercurial and, it seems, merited. In the next seven years he saw action on both sides of the Atlantic, mostly in combat with the French, and achieved the rank of commander. He was in charge of a ship called *HMS Amazon* for eleven years, initially under Admiral Lord Nelson, trailing the French fleet to the West Indies. He was in this area at the time of the Battle of Trafalgar and so did not take part in that encounter, although he was active off the coasts of Spain and Portugal soon afterwards. It is hard to imagine what the mood must have been like at Newton Hall at the time, with at least two of George's sons involved in what appeared to be almost ceaseless military campaigns. No doubt there was a good deal of trepidation — sadly borne out by what happened to Edward a few years later — but also a strong sense of pride as news of their achievements filtered through.

During a three-month period of leave in 1810, William married Frances Biddulph (see Family Tree I), daughter of Sir Theophilus Biddulph of Birdingbury in Warwickshire, before returning to his ship in European waters. In 1812, *HMS Amazon* was retired and the crew paid off. Now a wealthy man, William took the opportunity to purchase Shenstone Lodge, near Lichfield, where he and Frances lived a quiet country life for the next fifteen years. Their first son, William Biddulph Parker, was born there in 1824. However, three years after that their second son —

another George — was born at Newton Hall, as later census records show. The reason for this can only be a matter of conjecture. It is documented that William returned to naval duty in the Mediterranean in 1827, shortly after or possibly even before George was born. Perhaps it was felt in the circumstances that Frances, with two young sons to care for, would be better placed in the company of William's surviving sisters.

The following year, William took command of the royal yacht, *Prince Regent*. In the next three decades, he continued to excel in his duties, protecting British interests in war-torn areas such as the Far East (after his prestigious appointment as commander-in-chief in China), the Mediterranean and the English Channel. Such was the level of confidence in the Mediterranean fleet under his command that, for many years afterwards, people referred to a state of unparalleled perfection that was 'done in Old Billy Parker's time'.[23] This culminated in his appointment as admiral of the fleet in 1863 (fig. 18), when Queen Victoria sent him a private message saying 'it was well-earned reward for brilliant services'. He died three years later from a bronchial condition, being buried at his local parish church at Shenstone and commemorated, like his mother, in Lichfield Cathedral. There is an 'Admiral Parker Drive' (fig. 19) in Shenstone today, in memory of its most famous son.

William's naval career has been well-documented, most notably in a three-volume biography written by his friend and colleague, Sir Augustus Phillimore. There are few references to his family life, however. A fleeting exception appears in the middle of the second volume in a letter sent by William from his ship docked in Portugal to

Sir James Graham, First Lord of the Admiralty, on 12th April 1834. In it, he writes, 'An English vessel called the *Ellen Jenkinson*, lately arrived from Liverpool, bringing for me, in the private care of the Master (and not included in the manifest), a small present of some home-made ale (about 24 gallons) and cheese, from some female relatives who live near Chester.' It seems this vessel had been seized for non-payment of duty on these items, without prospect of release. William states that he had referred the matter to Lord Howard de Walden, British Ambassador in Portugal. He also says that there were precedents for transporting such goods in this manner. Whether the ladies of Newton Hall were knowingly involved in a tax avoidance scheme cannot be established. However, in this instance, as the goods were impounded as well as the ship, it is unlikely that they would have been in a fit state for consumption once eventually released. Testimony from the mid-twentieth century refers to a brewery and dairy having existed in what was then a tool shed in the wing to the rear of the hall.[24]

The *Dictionary of National Biography* sums William up thus:

> No officer of Parker's day made so deep an impression on the navy, by reason, not of extraordinary talent, but of exceptional fixity of purpose. In his youth he was considered by St. Vincent and Nelson as a first-rate officer. As an admiral, his conduct was distinguished by skill and tact. But it was as a disciplinarian that he was best known, not only in his own time, but to the generation which followed him; strict but not harsh,

with a fervent sense of religion and zeal for the service, ever bearing in mind the example of his great-uncle, he made everything bend to his idea of what was right ... A physical and family peculiarity is perhaps of greater interest — the extreme longevity of himself and his lineal ancestors, who for five successive generations attained the average age of eighty-six.

Returning directly to Newton Hall, had the census-taker in 1821 been able to penetrate the Hesketh and Parker households, this history would have been much the richer for it. Despite that, we still have a reasonable view of the occupancy of Newton Hall through this period, and it is more directly connected with the Parkers than the Heskeths in extant documents. What is not entirely clear is precisely how contemporaneous the two families were in their presence in the area, if and how they co-existed within the precincts of the hall, and what the relationships were like between them. There is some evidence that the Hesketh and Parker daughters were involved with each other because the report on the *Flookersbrook, Hoole and Newton Female Friendly Society* event organised by Emma Hesketh in 1816 states that it was attended by the 'Misses Parker'. This would almost certainly have been Martha, Ann and Frances, and it may also have included Elizabeth with three-year-old Emma in tow.

Elizabeth's whereabouts after the deaths of her father and sister, Martha, in 1819 are unclear, but we do know from a letter conveyed to William's ship that she died in 1828.[25] Emma maintained some sort of presence at Newton Hall, as she appears there under her married name in later census records.

On 1st July 1834, at the age of twenty-one, Emma married the Reverend Henry Biddulph (see Family Tree J), Rector of Birdingbury, Warwickshire. Henry — seventeen years her senior — was the younger brother of Frances Biddulph, who had married Emma's uncle, William, twenty-four years earlier. The wedding, we are told, took place in Chester.[26] All of this is unremarkable until we learn that Emma had given birth to a daughter — Adelaide Emma — two months earlier, also in Chester. It is hard to imagine that there would not have been some embarrassment — and possibly even scandal — attached to this episode: a country parson siring a child out of wedlock with a close family member a generation apart.

How this came about and how it was dealt with can be surmised from the available facts. We know that Frances Parker, née Biddulph, must have lived at Newton Hall around this time because her son George was born there in 1827. After her husband returned to sea that year for a lengthy period, she is likely to have stayed, no doubt supported by her sisters-in-law in the rearing of her children. It is probable that Henry visited his sister at the hall and that this was how his acquaintance with Emma was established.

Adelaide was baptised at Henry's church in Birdingbury (fig. 20) — or Birbury, as it is sometimes called — on 26th June 1834 at a ceremony presided over by the Vicar of Lillington, a small nearby parish. Whether this event was publicised and whether Adelaide was overtly acknowledged as Henry's daughter within the community, or even within the Biddulph family, is an open question.

What reinforces the notion that Henry, Emma and

Adelaide did not lead a conventional family life is the fact that they were living apart at the time of the 1841 census. Henry was domiciled in his parish with three female domestic servants in his household; Emma and Adelaide were living at Newton Hall with Ann Parker, their aunt and great-aunt respectively, and were attended by five female and two male domestic servants.

Frances — George Parker's daughter — had died unmarried at Newton Hall the previous year. Her will was proved on 19th March 1841, with her brother William and sister Ann being amongst the chief beneficiaries. William's unmarried daughters also received legacies, which were subject to forfeit in the event of any subsequent marriage. Special mention was made of 'my dear niece Emma Susan Biddulph'. She was to be party to a share in profits and dividends from Frances's assets as well as a one-off payment of nineteen guineas. The bequest to Emma was made 'notwithstanding her present or any existing coverture', which refers to the subordination of her rights to her husband in marriage. In other words, Emma's marital status was not a bar to her inheritance, in contrast with her cousins' status in the will. Despite this, there appears to have been no ill-feeling towards Henry, as he was an executor and a recipient of a £10 bequest, as was his daughter Adelaide. Frances also gave the books 'left me by my father' to her sister Ann and, after her death, to William's daughters. These were clearly precious family heirlooms: it would be good to know if these books survive to this day and, if so, what other family history they reveal. Generous amounts were also left to the nephews, including the princely sum of £500 to John Parker Nuttall. The will records the fact that it was drafted by 'Ph

Humberston and Henry Purkiss'.

As we can see, the Parkers and the Biddulphs were closely connected through marriage. Like the Parkers, the Biddulphs had strong Staffordshire links. Their ancestors, Sir Theophilus Biddulph, the first baron, and one of his sons, Michael, were both MPs for Lichfield in the second half of the seventeenth century. Simon Biddulph, Sir Theophilus's younger brother, acquired Birdingbury Hall in 1687 and his grandson — another Theophilus — inherited the baronetcy when his great-uncle's direct line ended. He was the first of the five Sir Theophilus Biddulphs of Birdingbury. The last of these — Frances Anne and the Reverend Henry's brother — fought in the Battle of Waterloo in 1815 and served as High Sheriff of Warwickshire in 1849.[27]

At some point in the early 1840s, Ann, Emma and Adelaide relocated to Warwickshire. In 1851, we find Adelaide shown on the census as a fifteen-year-old scholar living with her father at the rectory in Birdingbury (fig. 21), along with a governess and four servants. Two facts of note here are that she was living apart from her mother and that her actual age on the date of the census was irrefutably sixteen, approaching seventeen just over a month later. It can be inferred that the Reverend Henry was keen to pass her off as younger than she was to avoid the suspicion that she had been born out of wedlock. This presupposes a cover-up stretching back through her youth and possibly to last for her entire life. The death index which records her passing in 1869 estimates her year of birth as 1836: two years later than it actually was. Considering Henry's profession, the social standing of the Biddulphs and the Parkers and the sensibilities of the time, this may not be too fanciful a conjecture.

In 1851, Ann Parker and Emma Biddulph were living together in Kenilworth, Warwickshire, a few miles from Birdingbury. This suggests permanent, or at least long-term estrangement between Henry and Emma and, by contrast, a strong attachment between Emma and her Auntie Ann. Perhaps Henry and Emma were sharing custody of Adelaide at this point and this was the main motivation behind the move south, at a time when cross-country travel was still difficult, particularly into rural areas. Ann is unlikely to have found it palatable to stay at Newton Hall, given the loss of her sisters and advancing age. She herself died in 1855 at the age of seventy-three.

In 1865, Adelaide married into the church, like her mother. Her husband, who was eleven years her senior, was the Reverend Humberston Skipwith, the eighteenth child of Sir Grey Skipwith Bt and Harriet Townsend. Sir Grey was born in Virginia, USA, as the son of wealthy plantation owner, Sir Peyton Skipwith, who had bought land near Mecklenburg in 1765 which he developed into the three-thousand-acre Prestwould plantation. Upon his death in 1805, the estate included 235 slaves, making it one of the largest plantations in Virginia.[28] This is not the last we will hear of this pernicious trade, which maintained and enriched elements of the British aristocracy for many generations.

The wedding between Adelaide and Humberston took place in her father's church in Birdingbury on 25th October 1865. Two years later, their only child, Alice Louisa Skipwith, was born. Sadly, two years after that — in 1869 — Adelaide died, at the age of forty-three, predeceasing her mother, Emma. In the 1871 census, we see Emma living at the rectory in Hamstall Ridware near Lichfield, with the Reverend Humberston Skipwith, now the rector of that parish, and her granddaughter, Alice. She is shown as a widow, the Reverend Henry Biddulph having died four years earlier. Alice lived into her late eighties, dying unmarried in 1954 in Leamington Spa, where she had settled many years before with her father and his second wife.

Although Ann, Emma and Adelaide based themselves in the heart of England in their later lives, a Chester connection subsequently arose in Adelaide's husband's family. The Reverend Humberston Skipwith's elder brother, Lionel, had a son called Francis, who was born in London but became a bank manager in Chester in the late nineteenth century. He married in the city in 1899, living initially in Eversley Park and then Curzon Park. Francis fathered three sons, two of whom carried the traditional family forenames of 'Peyton' and 'Humberston'.

Returning briefly to the Newton Hall of Ann Parker's time, there is one other individual who merits further mention. This is George Parker (fig. 22), her nephew and second son of 'Old Billy Parker', the distinguished admiral. Reference has already been made to his birth and early years in the company of his mother and his aunts at Newton Hall. He too was to pursue a naval career and rise through the ranks to a position of eminence, becoming an admiral himself. Possibly because of his occupation, most of his adult life centred on the south-west of England, in close proximity to naval dockyards.

In 1857, George married Anne Elizabeth Mackworth Praed, the only daughter of William Mackworth Praed, a barrister attached to Lincoln's Inn and well known on the western circuit. William died in 1859 and his widow built a fine house on the family estate at Cornwood in Devon.[29] In due course George and Anne inherited this property, along with the lordship of the manor, and it was here that they raised a family and lived out their natural lives.

Despite holding the same rank, George's naval career appears to have been less illustrious and well-documented than his father's. This may simply have been because he served in a time of relative peace. It seems that the role for which he was best known was Master of the Dartmoor Hounds, a post he held for many years. In 1896 his wife died, and in 1903, at the age of seventy-five, he remarried, this time to twenty-four-year-old Rachel Violet Holmes in Paddington, London. He died the following year.

In the later 1840s, Newton Hall was occupied by a stockbroker and land agent called Charles Townshend. A document contained within the Accounts and Papers of the House of Commons in 1846 shows him depositing £53,000 – a huge sum for the time – towards a railway subscription contract.[30] *Bagshaw's Directory of Chester* of 1850 lists 'Charles Townshend, sharebroker, Newton Hall'. As well as being a successful businessman in his own right, he was descended from noble stock. His great-great-great-grandfather was Robert Cotton, first Baronet of Combermere, whose mother Elizabeth was born into the wealthy Calveley and Cholmondeley families. Charles spent large periods of his life in Denbighshire and Parkgate but may have been attracted to Newton Hall by its proximity to the railway network, which was burgeoning at the time. He married Mary Barker in 1834 and their first daughter, Harriette, was born two years later and baptised at St. Peter's Church, Plemstall, once frequented by the Hurlestons.

By 1851 the family had moved on to Christleton. After that, they appear to have divided. In 1861, Charles was living in Gresford with their second daughter, Susan, whereas Mary was living with Harriette and her husband, Latham Wickham, in Twyford, Hampshire. Curiously, Latham's profession is noted in the 1851 census as 'Clergyman without cure of souls', which indicates a lack of pastoral responsibilities. By 1881, Charles, now a Justice of the Peace (JP) and County Treasurer, was back in Chester and reunited with Mary, as they are both listed as living at Upton Bank, which was the original name for The Oaks and the present-day clubhouse of Upton-by-Chester Golf Club. Mary died in 1882 and, by 1891, Charles had been joined at Upton Bank and in partnership as a land agent by his thirty-year-old grandson, Robert Wickham. Charles appears to have still been active in this field at the age of eighty-one. He died at Upton Bank in 1893, leaving effects valued at circa £26,000 to Robert and to Charles Coppack, accountant.[31] Harriette predeceased him and Susan, who was to live a further two years, seems not to have been recognised in the will.

Before leaving the Newton Hall of the early to mid-nineteenth century, there is a little further colour to add. There is a document held by Cheshire Archives and Local Studies dated 30th September 1836 entitled 'Covenant from John Hurleston Leche of Carden Park, esq., to Faithful Thomas gent., to produce deeds, 1756–1831, relating to lands in Newton by Chester'. There is no further detail on the background to this request, or the outcome of it, but it seems reasonable to assume that this related to Newton Hall and its environs. The initiator of the covenant would have been John Leche XVI – the grandson of Mary Hurleston and John Leche XIV. It can be supposed that he was inquiring into the Kilmorey title to the land, perhaps finding some justification in the fact that Mary's elder sister, Anne, did not marry into the Kilmorey family until ten years after his grandparents were married.

If any challenge was raised around title to the land by means of the covenant, it appears to have been unsuccessful, as ownership remained with the Kilmoreys after 1836. As an aside, Faithful Thomas is an interesting figure. He was a Chester-based solicitor and Deputy Keeper of Records at Chester Castle.[32] In this latter capacity he was heavily involved in the transcription of records for George Ormerod's *History of Cheshire*. He also owned three plots of land to the west of Newton Hall.

Faithful Thomas's holding is confirmed by tithe maps for the year 1841.[33] We can use the same source to gauge the size of Newton Hall and its grounds at the time, amounting to approximately sixteen acres. Whilst not inconsiderable in itself, this is less than half the area owned and occupied by Henry Hesketh and his family next door. Newton Hall and the fields and outbuildings attached to it are shown as being owned by the Earl of Kilmorey and occupied by the 'Misses Parker'. As already noted, Frances Parker had died the previous year, leaving Ann the sole-surviving sister. Either the map-makers' records had not caught up with this fact or Emma and

Adelaide Biddulph were encompassed in the generic title of 'Misses Parker'.

Once again, some significant developments took place in the city of Chester during this period. The medieval gate towers on the walls had long outlived their usefulness as defensive structures and were obstructing traffic and perambulation. The East Gate, Bridge Gate and Water Gate were all replaced in elegant Georgian style in the late eighteenth century, followed by the North Gate in the early nineteenth century, which included removal of the notorious city gaol. The castle was falling into disrepair and therefore was also substantially redesigned and extended, in the Gothic Revival style. It housed the new city gaol.

Improvements in transport included the first canals to be dug in Chester in the late 1770s and, around the same time, the introduction of turnpike roads, which cut the journey time to London to two days, compared with twice that a century before. George Parker, amongst many others, would have reaped the benefit of this. On the downside, the River Dee continued to gradually silt up, further reducing Chester's status as a port, despite civil engineering schemes to counter it. This would have been detrimental to the Heskeths' business interests, given their reliance on imported wine. Early canal-side developments included steam-powered cornmills and the leadworks, incorporating the Lead Shot Tower, which is still visible from Newton Hall today. The original output of lead shot provided ammunition for the muskets used in the Napoleonic Wars.

Browns of Chester in Eastgate Street was rebuilt in 1828 in the Classical style, and the Grosvenor Bridge was opened in 1832 by Princess Victoria, who would become Queen later in the decade. This would have been a momentous occasion for the city and its inhabitants, especially as the bridge boasted the largest single span of any stone bridge in the world at the time. It was also of strategic importance, as improved transport links from the Midlands to Holyhead were having a negative impact on the economy of the north Wales coast. From the 1840s, a railway network began to be established. One tragic consequence of this for Chester was the derailment of a train on an inadequately constructed crossing over the River Dee in May 1847, at the cost of five lives and many severe injuries. Despite this setback, progress continued to be made in the development of the network, including the opening of Chester Railway Station in 1848. From then on, the sights and sounds associated with this form of transport would be a feature of life at Newton Hall and the area around it.

The talk through this period would also have picked up on significant national and, indeed, global events, given Britain's increasing influence on the world stage. Towards the end of the eighteenth century, the American War of Independence and the French Revolution would have caused no little consternation. Developments at and beyond the turn of the new century were generally more positive from a British perspective and included the Act of Union with Ireland, victories at Trafalgar and Waterloo and the merciful abolition of the slave trade.

The rapid pace of the Industrial Revolution gave rise to pressure from the working class for improved representation and human rights, leading to the Great Reform Act of 1832 and the emergence of the Chartist Movement. This may have been viewed as a further threat to landed families such as the Heskeths and the Parkers but, generally speaking, Chester was less directly affected by the Industrial Revolution and associated unrest than many other towns and cities in the north-west of England. From a constitutional angle, the period was dominated by the long reign of George III (1760–1820), overlain with the Regency from 1811, and followed by George IV, William IV and Victoria.

4

The Mid- to Late Nineteenth Century

The 1851 census, taken on the night of 30th March that year, lists the inhabitants of Newton Hall as:

Name	Relation to head	Condition	Age	Occupation
Catherine M Humberston	Head	Widowed	70	Landed proprietor
Anne Humberston	Daughter	Unmarried	40	At home
Mary E Humberston	Daughter	Unmarried	29	At home
Eleanor Williams	Servant	Unmarried	29	Cook
Hannah Hill	Servant	Unmarried	25	Ladies' maid
Eliza Brown	Servant	Unmarried	26	Housemaid
Mary Winstanley	Servant	Unmarried	33	Housemaid
Mary Holmes	Servant	Unmarried	18	Kitchen maid

John Hunt	Servant	Unmarried	33	Butler
Richard Dodd	Servant	Married	50	Coachman
Joseph Dogherty	Servant	Unmarried	15	Footman

We see that the hall has become the residence of the widowed mother and unmarried daughters of the Humberston family and their domestic servants. 'Humberston' is a name that we have encountered twice before in different contexts. Firstly, Philip Humberston was one of the two solicitors involved in the administration of Frances Parker's will in 1841. He died in 1844 at the age of seventy-three, and Catherine is his widow. The second reference to 'Humberston' is in the Reverend Skipwith's Christian name. There is no obvious relationship between his parents and Philip Humberston's family, so the nomenclature may simply be coincidental. However, there is a Staffordshire connection that pulls in the other direction. Philip Humberston's mother, Mary Foyer, was born at Shenstone in 1741 and married his father, John Cawley Humberston, at nearby Colton in 1763. Adjacent to Colton is Hamstall Ridware where the Reverend Humberston Skipwith would become rector some years later.

Even though Philip Humberston did not live at Newton Hall himself, he is worth a mention in this narrative because his contacts and his legacy would have supported his family in doing so. His solicitors practice and family home in Chester was in Whitefriars, at the bottom of Bridge Street.[1] It appears that this is where his ten children were born (see Family Tree K) — Catherine Maria in 1799, who died the same year; Frances, in 1801; Catherine, named after her mother and deceased elder sister, in 1803; Mary in 1805, who died the following year; Hester in 1806, who died in 1826; Anne in 1808; Sophia in 1809, who died in 1839; Maria in 1811; Philip Stapleton in 1812; and Mary Elizabeth in 1818.

These dates are taken from ecclesiastical sources — most notably a memorial stone at the church of St. Mary's on the Hill in Chester — and they highlight repeated inaccuracies in ages in census data as far as this family is concerned. For example, we know that Catherine, the mother, was born in 1777 and would have been seventy-three rather than seventy at the time of the 1851 census.[2] The birth registration process as we recognise it did not come into effect until 1853, so ages may not always have been known and may have been speculated upon, as we saw in the case of the 1821 census. They may also have been contrived, for reasons best known to the information-provider.

If we look further at census records relating to Anne and Mary Elizabeth Humberston, who lived together at Newton Hall for almost all of the second half of the nineteenth century, they present a somewhat fluid picture in terms of the progression of their years. For example, between 1851 and 1881, Anne aged by thirty-three years and Mary by thirty-four. Within this period, Mary's ageing process was particularly erratic. She advanced six years between 1851 and 1861, fifteen years between 1861 and 1871, and thirteen years between 1871 and 1881. Between the 1881 and 1891 censuses they both aged by seven years to seventy-three and sixty-three, respectively, placing their dates of birth at 1811 for Anne and 1821 for Mary. It is reasonable to suppose that their gravestone (fig. 23) represents the most accurate indication of when they were born. Those dates are 13th August 1808 for Anne and 16th August 1818 for Mary, giving an age gap of ten years and closely reconciling with the 1881 census data.

In addition to the property in Whitefriars, Philip owned an ancestral seat at Gwersyllt in Denbighshire.[3] At the turn of the eighteenth century this had been the property of George Shakerley, father of Geoffrey, first husband of Anne Hurleston.

Catherine Humberston, née Cotton, was also born into landed gentry (see Family Tree L). Her great-great-grandfather was Thomas Lynch, who was Governor of Jamaica on three separate occasions between 1663 and 1684. His daughter Philadelphia inherited his properties there and, upon her death in 1758, bequeathed them to grandsons, including 'real estate [745 acres], stock of negroes and other estate'.[4] This obnoxious legacy bypassed her eldest surviving son, Sir Lynch Salusbury Cotton — Catherine's grandfather and fourth Baronet of Combermere, near Whitchurch — who was already independently wealthy through his late father's line. The Combermere estate — the site of a former monastery and occupying almost a thousand acres — was acquired by a Sir George Cotton after the Dissolution and stayed in the family until the early twentieth century. It remains privately owned and Grade I listed in the present day. Catherine's father, also George Cotton, was Dean of Chester from 1787 until his death in 1805. The surnames 'Cotton', 'Lynch', and 'Salusbury' reverberate in Christian names down the family line. One apt effect of this is seen when Philadelphia remarried in 1716 after the death of her husband Thomas Cotton the previous year. Her new husband was called Thomas King and their first son was christened 'Cotton King'.

George Cotton's eldest brother was Robert Salusbury Cotton, who inherited the baronetcy and became MP for Cheshire between 1780 and 1796. His son, and therefore Catherine's cousin, was Stapleton Cotton. Stapleton achieved the rank of field marshal in the British army and became first Viscount Combermere as a result of his military exploits. He saw active service, most notably in India and in the Peninsular War, including at the Battle of Orthez, in which Edward Parker died. Later, he became Governor of Barbados and Commander-in-Chief in the Leeward Islands, Ireland and India. The role for which Stapleton Cotton achieved the greatest recognition was commanding the Siege of Bhurtpore in India in 1826, which overpowered a fortress previously deemed impregnable and restored the raja to the throne of that embattled state. It was for this that his rank in the nobility was elevated to viscount. His statue, cast in bronze and mounted on a horse, can still be seen on a traffic island outside Chester Castle (fig. 24). After retirement from military service, he devoted himself to parliamentary and social duties. A reactionary Tory, he opposed Catholic emancipation, the Reform Bill and the repeal of the corn laws.

The military adulation and political profile of Stapleton Cotton masked his most abhorrent activity overseas. He too was a slave-owner. When mass compensation claims were settled upon emancipation in the late 1830s, he and his cousin Barbara Yonge jointly accounted for 420 slaves in St. Kitts and Nevis. The payout was £7,200, equating to more than £800,000 today, of which Stapleton took the lion's share. His interests and property in the West Indies derived from his mother, Frances Cotton, née Stapleton, whose father, James Russell Stapleton, and aunt, Catherine Stapleton, had substantial holdings there.[5] A growing awareness of his involvement in the slave trade has led to vociferous calls in recent times for his statue to be removed. This follows angry protests in Bristol and the toppling of the Edward Colston statue as part of the widespread backlash against historic perpetrators of racial crime and social injustice on an egregious scale.

Stapleton Cotton was closely connected with the Duke of Wellington, inheriting the position of Constable of the Tower of London on Wellington's death in 1852. He was known to the novelist, William Makepeace Thackeray, who satirised him as Sir George Tufto in the *Book of Snobs*, initially published in *Punch* and then in book form in 1848. The excoriating portrayal describes him as having 'distinguished himself publicly as a good and gallant officer, and privately for riding races, drinking port, fighting duels and seducing women'. It goes on to add that he was 'one of the wickedest and dullest old wretches' who ever strutted over the earth.[6] Stapleton Cotton died in 1865.

His elder sister, and therefore also Catherine Humberston's cousin, Frances, married Robert Needham, eleventh Viscount Kilmorey, in 1792. As we have seen, he was the son of John Needham, tenth Viscount, and Anne Hurleston. He and his heirs would therefore have inherited Newton Hall along with the Kilmorey title upon the death of the previous incumbent. It is quite possible that the Humberstons found their way to the hall through this connection. We see something of the strength of the relationship between the Humberstons and the Cottons in the continuity of the Stapleton name in the Humberston family line. Philip and Catherine's son, Philip, bore this as a middle name, for example.

Catherine's affluent family background goes some way to explaining why she is noted in the 1851 census as a 'landed proprietor', even though she did not own the property in which she lived. Her husband's will of 1844 makes reference to his ownership of land in Elton and houses in Wrexham, which were left to his son.

Examination of Catherine's family line reveals another connection with the Parkers. Her younger brother, James Henry Cotton — one-time Dean of Bangor — had a son called Henry James who also rose to high ecclesiastical office, in his case as Vicar of Lichfield Cathedral. In 1851 — around the time that the Humberstons were occupying Newton Hall — Henry was living at Owens Villa in Shenstone as a neighbour of William Parker and his family. The nature of the relationship between those neighbours is unknown, but it is hard to believe that two such eminent people living in a small village at the same time would not at least have been aware of each other. Later, Henry became rector at Dalbury in Derbyshire and appears to have retired to Chester, where he died in 1884. Indeed, his grave is adjacent to the Humberston graves in the churchyard at Holy Ascension, Upton.

One final connection between the Humberstons and previous occupants of Newton Hall can be found in the lineage of Catherine, once again, and Charles Townshend. They shared a common ancestor in Robert Cotton, first Baronet of Combermere, who was her great-great-grandfather and his great-great-great-grandfather. This makes it more likely still that the Humberstons became aware of the availability of Newton Hall through family networks rather than more commercial channels.

Four of the Humberston children married in the pre-Newton Hall days: Catherine in 1825 to the Reverend George Pearson (fig. 25), later of Castle Camps, Cambridgeshire; Maria in 1838 to Vincent Roger Corbet of Shawbury Park, Shropshire; Philip Stapleton (fig. 26) in 1840 to Elizabeth Hughes of Bache Hall, Chester; and Frances in 1847 to the Reverend Robert Yarker of Neston (see Family Tree M). The combination of these marriages and Philip Stapleton's partnership in and subsequent proprietorship of his father's business may have been the cause of the reopening of Philip Sr.'s will in the late 1840s. In addition, the original will had been drafted in 1832 and so was already dated at the time of his death in 1844. A copy deed dated 15th January 1860, held at the Shropshire Archives, provides specific details of the revised provisions.[7] There is no suggestion that there was any acrimony behind the move. On the contrary, it appears to reflect new assets coming to light, including those generated by Philip Stapleton's successful expansion of the business, and the desire for a fairer apportionment amongst the enlarged family.

The revisions included provision for William Hall Eccles, the surviving son of Sophia Eccles, née Humberston, deceased; confirmation that pictures, prints, books, plate, wine, horses and carriages etc were to remain the property of Philip's widow, Catherine, for the term of her natural life; and validation of a dowry due to Robert Yarker, consequent upon his marriage to Frances in 1847. Philip Stapleton also took the opportunity to close the accounts on his father's estate. The total value was £133,000, with the largest share being granted to him — by way of reward for and 'to render him independent of professional exertions' — and the remainder shared between William Hall Eccles, George Pearson, Anne Humberston, Vincent Roger Corbet and Mary Humberston. These six individuals are the parties to the deed, Catherine Jr. and Sophia's interests having been subordinated to their husbands, who had their own solicitors review and approve the arrangements.

As was the case with George Parker's will, the impression is reinforced of Newton Hall not just being a fine estate but also housing some valuable possessions, including family heirlooms and fashionable modes of transport. There are three references in the deed to the wine bequeathed to Catherine, including a final one in marginalia to say, 'No wine remains,' at the time the deed was sealed. This may be completely unrelated, but when the conversion work was undertaken in the 1990s a large stash of bottles was found buried in an area to the west of the hall in which the sump is now located. The marginal notes also confirm that the furniture is to be 'retained by Miss Humberston and Miss Mary Humberston' in the wake of their mother's death. The terminology here is interesting as it pointedly identifies the elder sister as the new head of the household.

There must have been real cause for optimism when Catherine and her daughters, Anne and Mary, moved into Newton Hall at the turn of the decade. However, this would have soon evaporated as tragedy and loss beset the family a few years later. In 1854, one of Catherine Jr. and

George's six sons, James Falconer Pearson, drowned off Llandudno at the age of eight. The following year, Frances died. Probate records show that, in addition to the marriage settlement included in her father's will, she left to her husband effects valued at approximately £20,000; an impressive sum to belong independently to a married woman at that time. In 1859, both Catherines died — the daughter at Castle Camps in June and the mother at Newton Hall two months later. In Catherine Sr.'s case, probate was granted a as follows:

> The will of Catherina Maria Humberston formerly of the City of Chester and late of Newton Hall in the County of Chester Widow deceased who died on 23rd August 1859 at Newton Hall aforesaid was proved at Chester by the oath of Philip Stapleton Humberston of Mollington Banastre in the said County Esquire the Son and the sole Executor. Effects under £25,000.[8]

She had been baptised in 1777 at the original St. Bridget's Church, which stood near the junction of Whitefriars and Bridge Street in Chester. This church was demolished in 1829 as part of the construction work on the approaches to the Grosvenor Bridge. Catherine is therefore buried and commemorated with her husband and predeceasing children at nearby St. Mary's on the Hill, beside Chester Castle. It seems that she was increasingly referred to as 'Catherina' in later life, perhaps to distinguish her from her daughter, Catherine, and this is how she is represented on a memorial tablet at the church.

From a more general ecclesiastical perspective,

Newton was still served by the parish of St. Oswald's, as well as falling within the broader ambit of St. John's in the city and St. Peter's Church, Plemstall. In 1838, Christ Church Chapel was built in Gloucester Street, becoming the district church for Newton, part of Hoole and part of the city of Chester. In 1872, the Newton and Hoole coverage transferred to the newly built All Saints Church in Hoole Road.[9] By that stage, the Humberstons were firmly committed to worshipping at Holy Ascension Church in Upton and continued to attend services there, even though it was marginally further away from Newton Hall than All Saints.

They would have made this choice for several reasons. Firstly, the Upton church was established considerably earlier, initially as a chapel-of-ease to St. Mary's on the Hill. The first Sunday service was conducted on 4th June 1854 by the Reverend Henry Ireland Blackburne (fig. 27).[10] He was the son of Emma Blackburne, née Hesketh, and the late Reverend Thomas Blackburne and may well have secured the commission through his mother's contacts in the area, perhaps including the Humberstons. Secondly, Philip Stapleton and his family were based at Mollington Banastre, which is roughly equidistant on the opposite side of the Upton church from Newton Hall, and they were known to frequent it too. Beside the church, Philip's fellow solicitor on Whitefriars, Thomas Helps, had just developed and inhabited the fine Upton Lawn estate, now part of Upton-by-Chester Golf Club. The initials 'TH' can still be seen in the gable of the lodge — the only surviving vestige of the estate — on the junction of Upton Lane and Earl's Oak. Finally, it would have been a short and pleasant journey down a section of Newton Lane and along

Wealstone Lane and Church Lane, with the mill in the distance, past the Cockpit and Victoria Hotel at Upton Cross, to a newly-built church designed by renowned Chester architect, James Harrison.

Whilst the Misses Humberston and, for a time, their mother established themselves in the leafy surroundings of Newton Hall, their brother was making his first moves in the political arena. His success in the legal firm and inheritance from his father had provided him with the financial security to do this. The grief he felt at the loss of his mother and sister in 1859 may have been offset somewhat by his election as a Tory MP for Chester that year. In covering this event, *The Victoria History of the County of Chester* describes Philip as 'a popular local man'.[11] The legal practice, which had relocated from Whitefriars to 29 Northgate by 1846, continued to trade after Philip's election to Parliament. One of its clients at the time was Chester Cathedral, as we see an entry in their accounts in 1860 for expenses amounting to £53,7s,6d which 'arose from the Dean and Chapter taking counsel's opinion as to the legality of appointments to livings while the Deanery was vacant'. Also in 1860, Philip Stapleton's only son, eighteen-year-old Philip Hugh, went up to Magdalene College, Cambridge from Eton to study law. He was admitted to the Inner Temple six years later.

A further family event of 1860 was the death of the Reverend George Pearson, widower of Catherine Jr. Although he was born in Lichfield and died at Castle Camps, he is likely to have been close to the Humberston family from, at the latest, early adulthood as he was based in Chester between 1814 and 1825, performing his ministry at St. John's and St. Olave's before becoming a minor canon at Chester Cathedral. Indeed, there is a reference in the *Cheshire Sheaf* to a meeting of the Chester Book Club in 1824 at which both 'Rev. Geo. Pearson' and 'Mrs. Humberston' were present. This may have been the medium through which George and Catherine Jr. made or developed their acquaintance.[12] Moving to the remote village of Castle Camps in 1825, hard on the heels of their betrothal, was a bold step but no doubt offered them stability and autonomy in married life. Whatever the motive, they settled and raised a family and George remained rector there for the thirty-five years up to his death.

Philip Stapleton Humberston's term as MP lasted until 1865 and was punctuated by a spell as Mayor of Chester in 1861. After his time in Parliament, he turned his attention to deeper involvement in Chester society and other aspects of public service. In 1866 he was instrumental in helping to form the Grosvenor Club, becoming its second president, in succession to Earl Grosvenor, the Whig politician. An indication of the wealth and status of this organisation is the premises they built beside the East Gate in 1881, which are now occupied by HSBC Bank. Another great Victorian architect, John Douglas, was engaged for this purpose.

Philip also became involved in military affairs, ultimately becoming Honorary Colonel of the Cheshire Regiment. An early and significant undertaking in this capacity arose from the Fenian Plot of 1867. This was a major rebellion aimed at furthering the cause of home rule for Ireland at a time when political efforts were foundering. Irish American officers, who were veterans of the American Civil War, took the organisational lead and had 2,000 men at their disposal, many of whom were Irish émigrés living in England. What they lacked was weapons, so a plot was fomented to seize them from Chester, following which telegraph wires would be cut and trains and boats appropriated to transport men and munitions to Ireland via Holyhead in preparation for a swift offensive on Dublin. In the event, the plot was betrayed and pre-emptive action taken. *The Victoria History of the County of Chester* tells us:

> The city's chief constable, the deputy mayor, the volunteer Major Philip Humberston and the head constable of the county police had already moved the volunteers' rifles to the greater safety of the castle, mustered the police, militia and volunteers and brought another 70 regular soldiers from Manchester.[13]

Philip Stapleton's financial standing would have been in no way damaged by marriage. His wife, Elizabeth Henrietta Hughes, was a granddaughter of the copper magnate, Edward Hughes, who was one the principal partners in the Parys Mine Company in Anglesey in the late eighteenth and early nineteenth century. He developed a magnificent estate at Kinmel Hall, near Abergele, which was inherited by Elizabeth's brother, Hugh Robert Hughes, upon the death of an unmarried uncle in 1852. Elizabeth herself passed away in 1876 and Philip appears to have chosen to remember her by commissioning a fine stained-glass window at Holy Ascension Church in Upton, which is still in situ today, accompanied by signage which reads:

> The Kempe Room. This room is named after Charles Eamer Kempe (1837–1907), the leading stained-glass artist of the Victorian Era. Many of our great cathedrals contain his work. The beautiful Annunciation window in this room was in 1873 created by Kempe as a memorial for the lives of Elizabeth and Catherine Humberston.

There are also two contemporary plaques, one of which is in Latin and reveals the date of Elizabeth's death in the words, 'In memorium Elizabeth Henrietta Humberston que obit octavo dic mensis August a.d. mdccclxxvi' — that is, 8th August 1876 — and a second which simply reads, 'In pious memory of Catherina Maria Humberston.' If the window was truly created to commemorate both ladies, it must date from later than 1873, as Elizabeth was still alive at that time. The references to Catherine are presumed to relate to Philip's mother rather than sister, who spent most of her life in Cambridgeshire. The use of 'Catherina' rather than 'Catherine' on the plaque appears to confirm this. The tribute reflects an appetite to keep alive her memory within the family and community, in a setting that would have been close to all their hearts. Elizabeth was buried in the Upton churchyard, where her grave can still be seen today.

One significant event that did take place in 1873 was the marriage of Philip Hugh Humberston, Philip Stapleton and Elizabeth's son, to Edith Caroline Ffoulkes. She was the daughter of John Jocelyn Ffoulkes JP of Eriviatt Hall, Denbigh, and granddaughter on her mother's side of Admiral Sir William Beauchamp Proctor Bt. He was active in the British navy at the same time as William Parker and, given the seniority and equivalence of their ranks, it is unlikely they would not have known each other. Edith inherited the Eriviatt estate, but not until 1898, when her father died. At the time of their marriage, Philip Hugh lived at nearby Glan y Wern, which, like Newton Hall, survives to this day and is Grade II* listed.[14] As an aside, the double 'f' at the start of 'Ffoulkes' appears to date back to legal writing in Middle English which then continued in the printed form. This is borne out by the appearance of the capital 'F' in wills referenced elsewhere in this narrative, where the name 'Frances', for example, is handwritten as 'ffrances'.

Anne and Mary Humberston continued to live quiet and presumably contented lives at Newton Hall, busying themselves with the affairs of the estate and playing their part in local village life. They are shown as 'annuitants' in the 1881 census and were clearly able to live well on their independent means. They were supported by five live-in domestic servants at this time. Horticulture was a big passion of theirs and they took pride in displaying the fruits of their labours at horticultural shows throughout the region. Anne in particular appears to have been an enthusiastic reader, interested in antiquity. Amongst the publications in her possession were Geoffrey Whitney's *A Choice of Emblems* (1866) and James Croston's *Historic Sites of Lancashire and Cheshire* (1883), a source of material for this book. It is tempting to entwine these flimsy threads and suggest that she too was interested in the history of Newton Hall.

The 1881 census does not confirm where Philip Stapleton, Philip Hugh and Edith were domiciled as they were on holiday on the Cornish coast when it was taken, in the company of their butler and valet. Instead, they are shown at the top of the guest list of *The Falmouth Hotel*, with the first five lines used to describe the 'Rank, Profession or Occupation' of the two men. Philip Sr. is detailed as, 'JP for Cheshire and Denbighshire and DL [Deputy Lieutenant] in same; Colonel 2nd Battalion Cheshire Rifle Volunteers', and his son as, 'JP for County Denbigh, LLB Cambridge University'. No doubt a good time was had by all.

The Humberstons' commitment to the local community in this period extended well beyond church matters. Upton St. Mary's School pre-dates the church in Upton, having originally been built in 1843. Indeed, it was a venue for church services on Sunday until Holy Ascension Church was built eleven years later. Some of these services may well have been attended by the Humberstons. The building that we now see on Heath Road, operating as a privately-owned day nursery, is not the original school. By the 1880s, perhaps because of the growing population in the area, it was deemed not fit for purpose. *Upton-by-Chester — A People's History* takes up the story:

> The old school was demolished in 1884 and on 24th July 1884, the cornerstone of the new building was laid by Miss Mary Humberston. The school and house were presented to the parish by the Humberstons of Mollington Banastre, to open on 16th April 1885. The new red-brick building, described as 'very handsome and commodious', had a single large schoolroom with a platform at one end. On 27th May 1885, an 'Industrial and Art Exhibition' was held in

participation with surrounding villages. Later, an infants' classroom was added at the expense of Miss Mary Humberston, and in 1896, it was further enlarged.[15]

This passage captures a wonderful gesture by the family and clearly marks Miss Mary out as the most active member of it in the community at that time. The opening in 1885 must have been a grand occasion, with the Duke and Duchess of Westminster invited to attend. The school remained open for over a century, becoming an infant school for under-sevens in 1947, when the primary school on Upton Lane opened, and eventually closing its doors in July 1998.

This was a difficult period for the family too. In September 1883, Philip Hugh died at the age of forty-one, predeceasing his father. Despite his main residence being Glan-y-Wern, he maintained strong connections with the Newton and Upton areas and, like his mother, was buried in the churchyard at Holy Ascension. His will was proved on 20th November 1883 by his cousins, Philip Pennant Pennant of Nantlys, Flintshire, and Robert St. John Corbet, who lived in Lower Seymour Street, Mayfair — respectively the sons of Catherine and Maria. He left an estate valued at £8,736. In this context, the reference to 'the Humberstons of Mollington Banastre' at the time of the opening of the school in Upton in 1885 is an interesting one because Philip Stapleton — a widower who had lost his wife and only child — would have been the only surviving member of the family living there by that date. It is therefore more likely to be an expression of the more general associations made between the family and the

Mollington estate and, it is imagined, the extent to which Philip Stapleton's sisters, living locally at Newton Hall, spent time there.

Another question that arises here relates to the curious nomenclature of Philip Pennant Pennant, with the repetition of 'Pennant' and the absence of 'Pearson', his family name. Through his father's maternal line, he was related to David Pennant of Downing in Flintshire, who was also his godfather. David Pennant died in 1841, leaving substantial property to the only surviving member of his direct line: his granddaughter Louisa. She later married but died without issue in 1853, at which point her grandfather's estate, under the terms of his will, devolved to Philip Pennant Pearson. Part of this inheritance included properties at Bodfari and Tremeirchion. Philip chose to live at the splendid country house *Brybella* at Treimerchion before commissioning the building of finer property still on his land at Nantlys, which was completed in 1874. Here was hung a full-length portrait of Philip. He must have enjoyed and felt a strong kinship with the Pennant family because, in 1860, in the immediate aftermath of his father's death, he changed his surname to 'Pennant'.[16] His mother, as we recall, had died in 1859.

The signature of Anne Humberston of Newton Hall, amongst many others, appears on a fascinating document of 1889 which petitions the *London and North Western* and *Great Western Joint Railway* companies to create an access point to Chester Railway Station directly from the Hoole side of Hoole Bridge. The list of people who put their names to the petition includes many noteworthy individuals living in Hoole, Newton and Upton at the time, such as George Brown, six times Mayor of Chester and director of *Browns of Chester* department store; Earl Kilmorey; and George Dickson of the substantial Newton-based business, *Dicksons' Nurseries*. Charles Townshend, now living at Upton Bank, also features. The document itself sets out the case in robust terms:

> Several of your memorialists [signatories] are merchants, commercial travellers and others whose avocations necessitate daily or frequent railway travelling. At present, to get to the general railway station from this northern side, foot passengers must go past the station up the whole ascent of a long and disagreeable bridge, thence down a flight of steps which are only used on sufferance and are very uninviting, especially at night, and thence about 200 yards along a road on the south side of the station, which is frequently in almost unusable condition, and has no flagged, or other, footpath, whilst vehicular traffic has, in addition, to descend the bridge, make a sharp and dangerous turn, and return on a different level to nearly the starting point, thus accomplishing a wholly unnecessary distance of about quarter of a mile; moreover, the bridge, which has to be thus traversed for its whole length by buses and vehicles, and for the greater portion of its length by foot passengers, is subject to very heavy goods and cattle traffic. There is no protection for pedestrians against cattle being driven on it; it is very indifferently lighted at night, and it is subject to high shrieking, whistling, smoke and nuisances incident to a number of railways concentrating under it, as they run into the station. Your memorialists, therefore, very respectfully, but most urgently, ask

you to provide direct access to the station on the north side.[17]

Local people reading this in the present day may sympathise with these arguments as many of them still apply today, and there is a strong groundswell of opinion in favour of widening Hoole Bridge or combining it with a footbridge. However, what the 1889 petition requested was in fact delivered a few years later. The main catalyst appears to have been the 1893 Royal Agricultural Show, which was held on land in Hoole now occupied by Alexandra Park, Coronation Playing Fields and some of the surrounding streets. This was the biggest agricultural event in the world at the time and was a huge coup for Chester, and Hoole in particular. The volume of railway traffic surrounding the event necessitated preparatory work on the station and its surroundings. This included the creation of the access point on the Hoole Bridge and a dedicated ticket office for anyone using that means of entry. This work was only undone in the 1960s, when the now-dilapidated ticket office was demolished and the access point bricked up. It had served a valuable purpose, not least at the time of the Royal Agricultural Show, which welcomed well over 100,000 visitors, including Edward, Prince of Wales, who would later become King Edward VII. It is very likely that the Misses Humberston — keen horticulturalists, as we have seen — were present at the show, assuming their health permitted. They would also have had the opportunity to witness the crowds swarming up and down Hoole Road from the upper floors of Newton Hall.

In January 1891, Philip Stapleton Humberston passed

away and was buried in the same plot as his wife at Holy Ascension. There is an ornate gold plaque on the west wall in the nave of the church which reads:

> In memory of Philip Stapleton Humberston of Mollington Banastre. Hon Col. 2nd Vol Batt Cheshire Regiment, MP for Chester 1859-65. Born Aug 17 1812. Died Jan 16 1891. Col. Humberston by his will bequeathed the sum of £500 for the maintenance of this churchyard.

The bequest to the church was another fine gesture on his part and, in making it, he would have also had in mind the upkeep of his son's grave — adjacent to his wife's — and plots set aside nearby for the remains of other family members. Philip died at Glan-y-Wern, his late son's former residence, but is more directly identified in probate records as having lived at Mollington Banastre. He left an estate valued at £55,000 and his will too was proved by Philip Pennant Pennant and Robert St. John Corbet, along with George Falconer Pearson, all of whom were his nephews. The precise cause of death is not known but low temperatures may well have been a factor. The winter of 1890-1891 was notoriously harsh, with the River Dee freezing over for five and a half miles of its length. The funeral would have been a raw and difficult occasion for the ageing Anne and Mary Humberston, making their way across from Newton Hall, and for other surviving family members travelling from farther afield.

Aside from personal loss, the Misses Humberston continued to enjoy a quiet, stable existence at Newton Hall in the 1880s and early 1890s. The censuses for those decades show that they kept a household staff of five, occupying the roles of cook, ladies' maid, housemaid, kitchen maid and butler. Only Harriet Sadler, the ladies' maid, retained her post from 1881 to 1891.

In January 1894, at the age of eighty-five, Anne died at Newton Hall. Probate was granted the following month to her sister, Mary, and once again to nephew, Philip Pennant Pennant. Her estate was valued at £22,000. She too was buried at Holy Ascension, Upton, in a grave close to her brother and his wife, and beside her nephew, Philip Hugh Humberston. The grave is raised slightly above the ground and her name and dates of birth and death are inscribed along one of the bevelled edges. The corresponding edge on the opposite side would be marked with the same details relating to Mary when she passed away a little over twelve years later, at the age of eighty-seven. Mary had lived out her days at Newton Hall and left her estate valued at £20,000 to her nephew, the Reverend Edward Lynch Pearson. Almost half a century after Catherine Pearson's death, her sons were still receiving Humberston legacies. Mary had maintained the same number and configuration of staff at Newton Hall into the new century, with Harriet Sadler and Henry Jones, the butler, still in post in 1901.

A visit to Holy Ascension churchyard today will reveal a section immediately to the south and west of the church which is well-populated with Humberston family graves from the late nineteenth and early twentieth century. Most of these have already been mentioned, but they also include Philip Hugh's wife, Edith, who died in 1936 at the age of eighty-eight, and her two unmarried sisters, Cecilia and Constance Ffoulkes, who died in 1935 and 1950 respectively. They both appear to have lived locally, reinforcing the impression of a concentration of extended family in the area for a period spanning a hundred years.

An 1898 Ordnance Survey map of Newton (fig. 28) reveals an annexe adjoining the rear of the hall and the lodge at the entrance to what is now Newton Hall Drive, neither of which existed when the 1840 map was produced. The other significant addition to the landscape is the railway line, which dovetails with Newton Hollows and now forms part of the Chester Millennium Greenway.

The Misses Humberston lived at Newton Hall through a time of constitutional stability under Queen Victoria but enormous social change. In common with the nation at large, the population of Chester was expanding, despite the disappearance of traditional industries such as leather, linen and shipbuilding and the absence of a spate of factory-building. New suburbs such as Boughton and Queens Park were developed for the professional middle-classes and there was a rise in urban poor, housed in congested courts behind the main streets in the city centre. Chester's Irish population swelled significantly as a result of the famine years of the 1840s, and outbreaks of cholera and other infectious diseases were particularly rife in the middle of the century. Concern grew about drunkenness and anti-social behaviour, culminating in a riot in March 1882 when the Salvation Army paraded its brand of religion and strict temperance through the city. They were met by a mob with very different values, who resorted to sporadic acts of violence and were only dispersed by police reinforcements.

Construction work in the third quarter of the century

delivered the Grosvenor Museum, Grosvenor Park and the new town hall. The cathedral was also restored and extended at this time, under the direction of the renowned architect, Sir George Gilbert Scott. The turrets on the cathedral tower were a final addition to ensure it remained the tallest structure in Chester after the town hall achieved that accolade in 1869. The Misses Humberston would have witnessed much of this construction work taking place in the distance from the west-facing windows of Newton Hall. It is also highly likely that they attended a number of grand openings through this period. They would have seen or at least been acutely aware of damage and destruction to iconic buildings too. For example, in 1862 the old Exchange in the Market Square burnt down, giving rise to a competition to design the new town hall, and in 1881 the tower at St. John's collapsed, never to be rebuilt. A major focal point for cultural entertainment was Chester Music Hall, which opened in 1855, after a building standing between Northgate Street and St. Werburgh Street was revamped for the purpose. Early performers included Charles Halle, pianist and conductor, and the novelist, Charles Dickens, who visited on three occasions in the 1860s to give readings and lectures about his work.[18] These events may well have appealed to the Humberston tastes.

At a national level, the political stage was dominated by Gladstone and Disraeli and the main issues of the day included free trade and home rule for Ireland. The Empire appeared stable and secure and was protected by initiatives such as investment in the Suez Canal and conflicts in Crimea and the Transvaal. At home, Church of England evangelism and a series of Education Acts fostered a boom in church and school building, and we have seen how the Humberstons participated in this. Despite the booming population, a greater proportion of people lived in houses made of brick and stone, and paved streets, water mains and sewers were commonplace. Many homes had gas and even electricity at the turn of the century, by which time motorised transport was no longer a novelty on the roads. The railway network was mature and extensive, bringing renewed prosperity to Chester and leading to significant expansion in towns elsewhere in the county, such as Crewe and Birkenhead.

Whilst, to many, these developments would have represented progress and cause for optimism, this view was not universally held. The *Cheshire Sheaf* chronicler who provided such a graphic account of the 1821 census adds some personal reflections as he looks back from his vantage point in 1880. He takes as his pretext the life of Anne Brown, mother of Charles and William Brown, who ran the family department store so successfully during that period. She lived for many years at Newton Cottage, which was just north of Newton House, forming a fine triumvirate of properties with it and Newton Hall. Here is what he says:

> She is returned at this time [1821] as aged 31; and as she only died in 1879, she had continued to live in Newton for eight and fifty years ... What a story she could have told of the Newton of former days when four in hand coaches were passing to and fro along the Hoole Road; and lovers could visit the Hollows without being frightened to death by the shrill whistles of the puffing and smoking locomotives that

have done so much towards destroying the beauties of that once sweet and rustic neighbourhood. She passed the even tenour of her widowed life in that old home where her children were born and when her remains were reverently borne away to their last resting place by her sons and grandson it may be said the old history of Newton died with her; for the very men and women of 1821, whom she knew as residents there, had all been gathered to their fathers and the place that once knew them so well shall know them no longer for ever. Long before this nineteenth century will have reached its close there shall be no more Newton by Chester for Census takers to busy themselves with for Chester itself will have swallowed it up in its own municipal maw, and the very hollows will have been sacrificed to the builders' schemes 'civilising' that part of Chester by means of brick and mortar! Truly, we are at best vanity of Vanities and our once loved homes are indeed no better![19]

5

The Early to Mid-Twentieth Century

A combination of the *Chester Directory*, *Kelly's Directory* and the 1911 census informs us of a C. P. Smith occupying Newton Hall between 1907 and 1911. The census reveals this to have been Cecil Plumbe Smith, thirty-seven-year-old solicitor, who was born in nearby Mollington. In 1911, he was living with his thirty-eight-year-old wife, Mary; a housemaid, Dinah Jones; and seven members of the Clay family, who were predominantly domestic servants, including four committed to gardening duties. The lodge was occupied by the Jones family, the head of which was forty-four-year-old William, who was coachman at Newton Hall. It seems that the Joneses had followed the Smiths to the hall from their former home at Blacon Point, as they are shown as living in the lodge there in the 1901 census.

Cecil was a partner in the Chester-based law firm *Walker Smith Way*, located in Abbey Gateway. Any presumption arising from his surname that he was a founding partner is dispelled by the fact that the firm is mentioned in the 1889 petition for access to the station, when he would have been fifteen. Furthermore, we learn from *Cheshire Live* that when the firm went out of business in 2018 – three years after having been acquired by *Slater and Gordon* – it had been trading for over 170 years, placing its origins in the 1840s.[1] Nor was it a family firm; or at least it was not connected with Cecil's immediate line, because his father was a woollen draper. The reference to *Walker Smith Way* in the 1889 petition shows them to have been acting as agents for the local landowner, Lord Kilmorey. If this relationship continued into the new century, it is quite conceivable that this is how Cecil became aware of the availability of Newton Hall, following the death of Mary Humberston, and the opportunity to take up residence.

The Smiths lived at Newton Hall until just before the outbreak of the First World War, when they moved to Folly House at Flookersbrook. This was a prominent building, which was originally designed to be a windmill and which stood for 250 years. In 1860 it was acquired by Charles Brown, of whom we have already heard, and he further developed it. It passed to his daughter, Lucy Elizabeth, upon his death in 1900, and she lived there until the Smiths took it on. Their occupancy ended in the 1930s, when the property was demolished and the houses now located in Fieldway and Sandileigh were built.[2] The Smiths' presence at Folly House is a further indication of their financial heft, which was enhanced by the sale of land upon which Alexandra Park in Hoole was created. They too were active in the local community, with Mary serving as Commandant of the Cheshire 46 Red Cross Detachment and Matron of Hoole Bank House Auxiliary Hospital.

At some point during or shortly after the First World War, Mrs. Margaret Frost moved into Newton Hall, remaining in residence up to 1923.[3] She was the widow of James Garrett Frost, who had been Mayor of Chester in 1901 and 1902 and a long-standing director in the family flour-milling business F. A. Frost & Sons, based at the Steam Mill in Chester and later in Ellesmere Port. His father, Robert, had been responsible for the expansion of the business in the latter half of the nineteenth century, building on the success of his own father, Francis Aylmer Frost, who first established it in 1814. Robert was Mayor of Chester three times in the 1860s and 1870s and had the honour of laying the foundation stone for the new town hall in 1865. He invested some of his fortune in property in the local area. This included Linden Grove, on the banks of the River Dee in Queens Park, and the thirty-room mansion of Boughton Hall (fig.29) on the south-east fringes of the city. James was to benefit from these properties upon his father's death in 1895 and occupied Boughton Hall with Margaret in the early years of the twentieth century.[4] Here he hosted dinner parties during his term as mayor as well as being noted for the scale of his hospitality at the town hall itself, where impressive balls were held.[5]

Robert Frost had married his cousin Jane, who was the daughter of his uncle, James Garrett Frost. The James Garrett Frost who married Margaret — later resident at Newton Hall — consequently had a namesake in his grandfather through his mother's line and great-uncle through his father's. As we have seen with other families, intermarriage took place and forenames perpetuated down the generations. Margaret was the daughter of W. A. Hills, a Ramsgate-based solicitor, and niece of Dr. William Stubbs, an eminent historian and Bishop of Chester between 1884 and 1889. The wedding between James and Margaret in October 1885 was a grand occasion, presided over by Dr. Stubbs.

James and his cousins John and Thomas, in addition to being hard-working businessmen in the family firm, were committed rowers. In 1892, they were part of the 'eight' who won the Thames Challenge Cup at Henley, receiving a hero's welcome on their return to Chester. James and Margaret had two sons and three daughters, born between 1886 and 1901. Another James Garrett Frost was the youngest. He appears to have been born on the day of the census as his age is recorded as '0 hrs'. James Sr. died from typhoid in 1912 at the age of fifty-two at a property in Stanley Place, his presumed town house in Chester.

With Boughton Hall and other options at her disposal, the question arises as to why Margaret chose to live at Newton Hall. It could be that proximity to members of the extended family was a factor. Upton Lawn, erstwhile residence of Thomas Helps, was now owned and occupied by John Meadows Frost, her late husband's cousin and his second wife, Dora. John was a noteworthy figure in Chester at the time as he was in the process of becoming the city's longest standing mayor; an office which he held from 1913 to 1919. He was knighted for his public service and clearly had a reputation and network which extended well beyond the local area. One of his guests shortly after the end of the war was none other than Earl Haig,

Commander of the British Expeditionary Force on the Western Front from 1915 to 1919. This must have been a bitter-sweet occasion for Sir John as he had lost his second son, Laurence, in front-line combat at Ypres in 1915. Perhaps devastating wartime absences and impacts such as these reinforced the bond amongst the elder generation of the family.

Sir John himself lived on until 1935 and is buried in the family grave at Holy Ascension Church in Upton, not far from the Humberstons. As a popular and generous contributor to the local community, he is further commemorated in the street name 'Meadowsway', which runs off Upton Lane, close to the former location of Upton Lawn. In the period 1924–1925, Sir John's eldest son, Hugh Kelsall Frost, is recorded as living at Newton Cottage, though it is unclear when he first took up residence there. The cottage had been occupied during the First World War by a Miss Clark-Jones, who was host to the family of the Emperor of Abyssinia and governess to his daughter.[6]

Whatever it was that attracted Margaret to the local area, she stayed until her own death in 1941, as probate records reveal her address at that time to have been 'Homefield, Liverpool Road, Chester'. *Kelly's Directory* of 1934 shows her residing at that address and serving as a JP and has her son Robert living in nearby Eversley Park. Upon her death, he was the first-named beneficiary of her estate, valued at £17,154. Six years later he too would become Mayor of Chester, maintaining a long-standing family tradition in that vein.

Confirmation of Margaret Frost's occupancy of Newton Hall up to 1923 is provided by *Kelly's Directory* of that year. However, a copy of the directory for the previous year held at Chester Reference Library includes a curious emendation in that 'Frost, Mrs J G [John Garrett, her late husband]' is crossed out by hand and the words 'Evill, 11 Tithebarne St, Liverpool' inserted alongside it. There is no mention of the forbidding-sounding 'Evill' in 1923, but the directories for 1924–1925 and 1925–1926 list F. E. Evill as the occupant of Newton Hall. This implied cross-over between Frost and Evill suggests a period of co-habitation, or at least some type of relationship between them. However — other than a record of a thirty-two-year-old lady by the name of M. E. Evill arriving in Liverpool on 18th January 1925 bound for Newton Hall, Chester, after travelling second class on a passenger ship from Karachi — the trail on the Evills goes cold.

In 1926, Alfred Kenney Tyrer and his wife Rachel (see Family Tree N) moved into Newton Hall along with their three teenage daughters, and they remained in residence until the early 1940s. He was known as 'Kenney', presumably to distinguish him from his father (fig. 30), with whom he shared the forename 'Alfred'. His grandfather William, a Liverpool-based solicitor, also had the middle name Kenney, which was derived from the maternal side of his family (see Family Tree O). William's mother, Christiana, first married an Edward Rogers Kenney and, after his death in 1808, married David Tyrer in 1813. William was a product of this marriage two years later. Christiana and Edward had had a son, also called Edward Rogers Kenney, in 1801.

It seems that the Tyrer and Kenney families were firmly and successfully embedded in the legal profession in Liverpool over several generations, specialising in bankruptcies. Edward Jr. was a solicitor, as was Alfred, William's son.

As affluent and prominent Liverpool-based businessmen in the early nineteenth century, perhaps it comes as no surprise to learn that some of their wealth was ill-gotten through slavery and plantation interests. Edward Jr.'s elder sister Frances married Paul Massiah, who was a merchant and trader based in Georgetown, British Guiana. William and Edward Jr. were trustees for the Massiah's minor children, and, in 1836, Edward acted as agent in requesting that his slavery compensation money be used to develop a property in Georgetown. The freeing of six enslaved people equated to the sum of £267,19s,9d.[7] Whilst Massiah did not operate on the same scale as other slave traders we have encountered, his mere involvement in this opprobrious business remains a deep scar on him and his family line.

William Tyrer died in 1875 in Geneva, though probate records show his residences to have been in Liverpool and Sutton, on the south-east fringe of the Wirral peninsula. He therefore had a presence a few short miles away from Newton, where his family were soon to plant their roots. His estate was valued at the colossal sum for the time of approaching £100,000. As his only son, Alfred benefitted greatly from his legacy. At the age of twenty-five, Alfred was establishing himself in the legal profession, becoming a partner in the firm *Tyrer, Kenion & Simpson*. He married Elizabeth Ida Burton in 1877 and by 1881 they were living in Knotty Ash, Liverpool, with their three young children, the eldest of whom was Kenney, aged three. Later in the 1880s, they moved to Plas Newton in Chester, just to the north of Newton Hall.

There was a trend from the mid-nineteenth century onwards for some affluent Liverpool-based businessmen to choose to live in the Newton and Upton areas, attracted by the improved transport links engendered by the railways. Other examples include Robert Roberts, tea merchant of The Firs and his son Benjamin Chaffers Roberts, who took on the business and built Oakfield, now part of Chester Zoo; Edward Logan, copper merchant, who followed Thomas Helps into Upton Lawn; and, later, Sir Helenus Robertson of Upton Grange — adjacent to Upton Lawn — who was chairman of the Mersey Docks and Harbour Board. Despite the status of their owners and the grandeur of these properties, none of them could rival the magnificence of Plas Newton, the sprawling footprint of which can be seen in the map of 1898.

Plas Newton appears to have been built in the early 1840s by the family of Colonel Edward Evans-Lloyd, who hailed from Carmarthenshire. This explains the epithet 'Plas', which means 'large house or mansion' in Welsh. As well as having military connections, Edward Evans-Lloyd was a Chester-based solicitor, freeman of the city, and organist and warden at Holy Ascension Church, Upton for thirty years. He was a great fundraiser and philanthropist and, amongst other things, paid for the clock faces and mechanism of the Eastgate Clock, which carries the inscription 'THIS CLOCK WAS PRESENTED TO THE CITY BY EDWARD EVANS-LLOYD CITIZEN & FREEMAN 1897' (fig. 31). Both he and Alfred Tyrer were signatories to the 1889 railway access petition, with Alfred having taken possession of Plas Newton at that time. A good description of the property and its grounds is provided by the website *parksandgardens.org*:

Under the ownership of wealthy Alfred and Ida Elizabeth Tyrer, Plas Newton was a renowned country gentleman's estate ... Garden Parties and show prizes were the order of the day ... It had woodland with masses of daffodils and crocus surrounding a long drive. The lawn ended in a ha-ha giving views over the Welsh hills. A Japanese garden, summerhouses, topiary and pergola were amongst the many features. The outhouses and walled garden were extensive.

Bill Morgan, who moved to Plas Newton in 1925 as the two-year-old son of the newly-appointed head gardener, William Morgan, adds some further detail. He describes a putting green, an orchard, waterfalls, and figurines shipped directly from Japan. There was a cemetery for dogs and a large stable block. Garden parties were a regular occurrence, featuring huge marquees and the General Railway Station brass band for entertainment.[8] The house was full of valuable treasures, which were put up for auction after Alfred's death in 1946, attracting buyers from far and wide. After that, the estate gradually diminished. The last surviving vestige of this lost world was the stable block, which was accessed through a private driveway marked 'White Gables', just below Cheshire County Sports Club on Plas Newton Lane. This was a private residence for a while and, after falling into a state of complete disrepair, has only recently been demolished to make way for a new housing development on what is now 'White Gables Close'.

In some ways, it is fitting that the stable block lived on because Alfred Tyrer was passionate about equestrian activities. He reputedly played polo for England in his youth and he maintained an extensive stock of polo horses at Plas Newton. He was Honorary Secretary of Chester Polo Club and in 1894 secured the future of the club and its home on the Roodee. Writing in the book, *Polo,* the following year, J. Moray Brown tells us that the club had been in a parlous state until Alfred revived it, including successfully applying for council funding to level the ground, which markedly improved it as a playing surface. Plas Newton was the published address of Chester Polo Club worldwide.

A report in the *Chester Courant* of 12th August 1908 shows the Tyrers on a long but exclusive guest list for Eaton Polo Week, hosted by the Duke of Westminster. There is an 'A. Tyrer' in one of the competing sides, the Foxhunters. This is most likely to have been Alfred Kenney Tyrer as Alfred himself would have been fifty-eight years old at the time. The stables produced some notable racehorses too; one being Upton Lad, which was ridden by Billy Dutton in the Grand National of 1927. The following year Billy won the event riding another local horse, Tipperary Tim, with a starting price of 100-1.[9]

Other indications of the trappings of Alfred's wealth appear in the records. For example, in September 1911, he sailed on the *Lusitania* from Liverpool to New York, bound for Calgary in Canada. This was in the halcyon days of transatlantic travel, before the sinking of the *Titanic* seven months later and the outbreak of the First World War, during which the *Lusitania* would be infamously torpedoed, with the loss of almost 1,200 lives. The ship's manifest for the journey that Alfred took contains some surprising information on him. When asked to provide

'The name and complete address of nearest relative or friend in country whence alien came', he responded with, '(Friend) Mr. H. Barnston, Farndon, Chester.' Why he chose not to mention his wife or family, none of whom were travelling with him, is unclear. His friend was in fact Sir Harry Barnston, first Baronet of Churton and a descendent of Trafford Barnston's family, into which Elizabeth Hurleston had married almost two centuries earlier. Perhaps Alfred felt his friend's social status would be helpful if there were any questions as to his bona fides. When asked whether he was joining a relative or friend at journey's end and, if so, what their full address was, he simply stated 'friends', being much more sparing with the detail than his fellow-travellers.

The First World War affected the Tyrers, as it did everyone. Oliver, the second son, was a lieutenant in the Royal Field Artillery, being wounded in action but thankfully not fatally.[10] It seems his war service ended in 1917, perhaps on medical grounds. In the same year, Alfred lent £20,000 to the war effort. In 1919, he became involved in the Upton-by-Chester War Memorial Committee and contributed £100 towards the construction of the monument. Amongst other connections, he was personally and professionally close to the Logan family, who lost two sons in the war, both of whom feature on the Upton war memorial. The younger son, Roland Logan, left a letter about the disposal of his assets *post mortem* which refers to 'Mr. Tyrer' and begins, 'You will only get this if the Germans get me.' Regrettably, they did. During the Second World War, the Tyrers suffered a more direct loss when their twenty-four-year-old grandson, William Paul, of the the Royal Welch Fusiliers — son of their daughter Ida —

died in 1940. He is commemorated on their grave at Holy Ascension, Upton.

Either side of his war experience, Oliver appears to have been something of a bon viveur and world traveller. He attended Eton between 1894 and 1897 and lists his occupation in the old boys' book as 'golf, polo, hunting and yachting'. In 1899, he was returning from New York to Liverpool as an eighteen-year-old 'gent' after five weeks in Montreal and in 1912 travelling from Vancouver to Honolulu. After the war he seems to have had a spell in New Zealand, describing his profession as 'solicitor' when he returned via Brisbane to Hull in 1924. In 1931, he travelled from Southampton to Jamaica and in 1932 he was sailing again between New York and Southampton, now in retirement. He died at Plas Newton two years later at the age of fifty-four, leaving effects of £1,190 to his father, whom he predeceased. This legacy represents quite a modest sum in the context of his family wealth and background.

Kenney Tyrer was born in 1878 and spent his early years at the family home in Knotty Ash before they moved to Plas Newton. He was the eldest child, being two years older than Ida and one year older than Oliver. In 1891 he was the sole child in the household as his siblings were away at boarding school in St. Peter Port, Guernsey. It is not clear where his schooling took place and, at the age of twenty-two in 1901, he was still living with his parents and with no profession or occupation recorded against his name in the census of that year. In 1906, he married Rachel Salkeld Robinson, the daughter of James Robinson, a JP and engineer from Rochdale. It seems that she had moved to Chester with her two sisters — following the death of both parents in the early 1890s — as they are shown in the 1901 census as living with an aunt at Abbots Park Lodge. Kenney and Rachel settled in Little Saughall, just outside Chester, as a married couple and the following five years blessed them with their three daughters. The census of 1911 lists Kenney's profession as 'engineer'. It is fair to suppose that his career choice is unlikely to have been directly influenced by Rachel's father, as he died when Kenney was thirteen, and it is questionable whether the two of them ever met.

There is a picture of Kenney and Rachel from this period (fig. 32) picnicking with another lady, possibly one of Rachel's sisters. They are elegantly clad in their Edwardian attire. It is not known precisely where the picture was taken but it is easy to imagine from the leafy setting that it was not far removed from their semi-rural home.

Kenney and Rachel would have been acquainted with the Humberston family and Newton Hall in their youth. The church and vicarage in Upton would have been the hub of social activity and the Newton Hall estate, which abutted Newton Lane, would have been more conspicuous at that time. The Humberstons' properties in Mollington and, through marriage, at Bache Hall and in the Liverpool Road area were all close to where Rachel lived in Abbots Park. Furthermore, the Hughes and Ffoulkes families appear on the guest list for Eaton Polo Week in 1908, at which the Tyrers featured prominently, as we have seen. Other guests included Harry Barnston; Colonel Evans-Lloyd; Mr. J. M. Frost, Upton Lawn; and Mr. and Mrs. J. G. Frost, Boughton Hall.

Kenney's status during the war is uncertain. There is

a record of a Sergeant Alfred Tyrer, who served in the King's Liverpool Regiment, but this may well have been someone else. As a thirty-eight-year-old engineer when war broke out, it is possible that his contribution was on the home front. The Tyrers' time at Newton Hall appears to have been relatively settled and uneventful. In 1934, Elizabeth — the eldest daughter — married Hugh Richmond in Chester and, a few years later, her sister Margaret married James Greenwood. In the Hoole District Register of 1939, Kenney and Rachel are listed at Newton Hall, along with Margaret and the middle daughter, Katharine. The surname 'Tyrer' is crossed out beside Margaret's name and 'Greenwood' inserted, suggesting her marriage was relatively recent, though it is unclear why she was not living with her husband. Kenney's occupation in the register is shown as 'Company Director' and Rachel's as 'Unpaid Domestic Duties'. With five domestic servants also listed, it is reasonable to suppose that Rachel's duties were not overly burdensome. Margaret and Katharine are noted as being involved with the 'Field Ambulance Nursing Convoy, 36th Western Branch', which may well have been mobilising at the time to support the impending war effort. It is not improbable that Newton Hall served as a makeshift hospital or base for evacuees during the Second World War, in common with similar properties in the area, but documentary evidence to that effect is lacking.

We are fortunate to have a short but vivid account of Newton Hall, and Kenney Tyrer in particular, from Bill Morgan, contained in his reminiscences in *Upton-by-Chester — A People's History*. He tells us:

I very often used to meet Mr Kenney Tyrer, who lived

at Newton Hall, taking his five dogs to Picton for their morning exercise. On these occasions I was expected to touch my cap, dismount, stroke the dogs and hand over my homework for scrutiny. He was a very keen cyclist and on one particular morning he informed me that I was to call at the hall on my way home from school in order to inspect his new bicycle that was being delivered from France that very day. The maid that answered the door, informed me that I was expected and I was ushered into the courtyard where a spanking new bicycle was standing upside down. At the point of me giving it my well-rehearsed praises, he informed me that it had to go back to the factory. 'Surely not? Why?' He spun the wheel and it eventually stopped with the valve at the top of the wheel. 'You see, my boy, it should have stopped at the bottom and so it proves that the wheels are not properly balanced.' And, indeed, it went back![11]

A lot can be inferred from this passage, including the fact that Kenney appears to have been a precision engineer. Bill also talks about the darkness around the hall during the wartime blackout and the consequent danger of colliding with one of the many large farmyard animals that still pervaded the area at that time. He adds that German prisoners of war were employed and Polish families housed in nearby fields towards the end of the war.

Not long after this, the Tyrers moved from Newton Hall to Lower Carden Hall. The catalyst for this may well have been Alfred Tyrer's death in 1946. Ida, his wife, had died four years earlier and Kenney was his only surviving son. He left the enormous sum of £245,000.

Lower Carden Hall still exists today as a Grade I listed

building and is just below and in the same parish as the former site of Carden Hall, which, as we have noted, burnt down in 1912, prompting the Leche family to relocate to nearby Stretton Hall. It is reported that the Leches had in their possession at Stretton Hall mid-eighteenth century portraits of Anne and Mary Hurleston.[12] The family left the property in the 1980s and, it seems, took the portraits with them. Their current whereabouts are unknown. Though entirely coincidental, there is a nice symmetry to the fact that Kenney Tyrer made the same move from Newton Hall to Carden as Mary Hurleston had done more than 200 years earlier. Kenney and Rachel both died there in 1952, with Kenney leaving an estate valued at £180,000.

Chester continued to change and develop through this period in a number of ways. The black-and-white Tudor revival initiated in the late nineteenth century, most notably around the Cross, persisted. A large-scale example of this is the St. Michael's Row building on Bridge Street, funded by the second Duke of Westminster. At first, the frontispiece was covered in cream ceramic tiles, some of which can still be seen at street level. Such was the traditionalist backlash when it was unveiled in 1910 that it was swiftly replaced with the huge black-and-white timber structure which also survives to this day. The shops and arcade behind it were developed at this time, further cementing Chester's position as an important retail centre in the region.

Inevitably, war dominated this period across the generations. The First World War had a deep and immediate effect on Chester, as the First Battalion of the

Cheshire Regiment was almost completely wiped out at the Battle of Mons in August 1914. Eaton Hall and Oakfield House were amongst the large country houses which became military hospitals or nursing homes at this time. At the end of the war, the memorial placed in the town hall by Mayor Frost — dedicated to his fallen son, Laurence — included the names of 771 men.

In 1920, the Music Hall, which had been screening films since the turn of the century, was fully converted to a cinema. Other cinemas followed in the 1930s in the shape of the Odeon on Northgate Street and the Regal on Foregate Street. The opening of the former in 1936 was a glittering occasion, with appearances by Douglas Fairbanks Jr. and the Jack Payne Band. It is easy to imagine the Tyrers and members of their social circle in attendance. In the same year, the borough boundaries were extended to include expanding suburbs, one of which was Newton. Excavation work began at the amphitheatre following its discovery in 1926 and the nearby re-modelled New Gate opened in 1938.

The Second World War saw a number of army camps established in the area and the mass production of Wellington and Lancaster bombers at Broughton. From May 1940 onwards, air raids by the Luftwaffe would have been a common feature of the night sky as it engaged in a savage blitz on Liverpool, the effects of which would have been audible and visible from Newton Hall. An anti-aircraft battery was stationed on Acres Lane, near the Zoo, and Chester itself suffered occasional hits, with resulting damage including shattered windows at the cathedral in November 1940 and a crater on Upton Golf Course in April 1941. In 1942, American troops arrived in the area, many of whom were stationed close to Newton Hall, at Hoole Bank House and the rugby club at Vicars Cross. They made quite an impression on the area for the duration of their stay, attracting their fair share of GI brides. In early June 1944, huge and clandestine troop movements took place, with massive convoys making their way south through Newton along the line of the A41. This was the prelude to D-Day, the Normandy landings and the beginning of the end of the Second World War.

The two World Wars, of course, had prodigious and far-reaching impacts around the world. Britain's influence within it was declining and the Empire was beginning to erode. The losses suffered in the First World War were compounded by an outbreak of Spanish flu in 1918 and 1919 with a death toll of 200,000 people in Britain alone, which has eerie resonance today, a little over a century later. Home rule and partition in Ireland came about in 1920 and the General Strike took place in 1926. The aristocracy and landed gentry faced new challenges as a result of greater emancipation, the emergence of the Labour Party and rising taxation. Many would have been impoverished by the Wall Street Crash of 1929 and the ensuing Great Depression. The stability of the monarchy embodied in Queen Victoria could not be maintained for long after her death in 1901. The abdication of Edward VIII in 1936 was a low point for the institution in the first half of the century. Transport continued to develop with the proliferation of motorised vehicles and the beginnings of passenger air travel. Buses became commonplace, replacing trams in the city of Chester in 1928. It is reasonable to assume that families such as the Frosts and the Tyrers were amongst the early adopters of the motor car and that these soon became a regular fixture in and around Newton Hall.

6

Mid-Twentieth Century to the Present Day

There is no intention to cover this period in detail, for two main reasons. One is that, for some people, it is within living memory, which belittles any account based on cold historical data. The second is that, in the middle of the twentieth century, the hall was first converted into flats, with a change in the character of the building internally and, in due course, more diverse occupancy.

A local architect, Robert Boot, bought the property from the Tyrers and undertook the conversion into six flats and four flatlets, with seven garages attached. One of his finds at the time was a tile bearing the ermine emblem of the Hurlestons, which may even have pre-dated Newton Hall.[1] The hall was sold in 1949 with vacant possession to George Edward Shaw — a biochemist — his wife Elizabeth and their family. The farm to the rear, in which the dovecote was situated, and the lodge at the foot of Newton Hall Drive were already separately owned at this time. The daughter of the Shaw family has kindly provided notes written by her mother; her mother's correspondence with Professor Kenneth Hurleston Jackson; photographs of the hall from this period; and sales literature from the 1960s and 1990s. All of these are relevant to the history of Newton Hall, particularly the research done by Elizabeth and Kenneth, which is referenced elsewhere in this book. George Shaw died in 1962, just a few weeks before his daughter's wedding at St. Peter's Church, Plemstall. The notion of a ceremonial procession between these two locations transports us back to the very earliest days of Newton Hall.

Photographs from 1950 of the lane and grounds are revealing (figs. 33 and 34). We see the rural character of the land immediately beyond the hall and how well-kept and well-stocked with trees, shrubbery and floral features the gardens were. Amongst other things, we get a sense from this of why the Humberston sisters may have taken such a keen interest in horticulture and of some of the generous and enticing space in which they would have pursued it. The gravel driveway, sweeping gently downhill through an avenue of lime trees with cattle grazing in the background, is a timeless image and a reminder of how little some aspects of the estate changed down the ages.

Kenneth Hurleston Jackson's interest in the property is implicit in his name. He was descended from Peter Hurleston, who was born in 1624, a younger son of the John Hurleston born in 1590. Kenneth was a leading authority on Celtic languages and held professorships at Harvard and Edinburgh. His letters focus on the make-up and movements of the Hurleston family in the late seventeenth and early eighteenth century and how they bear on the building of Newton Hall. One of his missives ends with the moving words, 'I suppose it is sentimental of me, but I do take a kind of ghostly proprietary interest in its fate, as my ancestors once lived there — and also because it is a beautiful house.' Reference was made at the start of this book to the fluidity in spelling of the Hurleston name. It is noticeable that the letters are signed 'Kenneth Hurleston Jackson' and yet in his many publications he is 'Kenneth *Hurlstone* Jackson'. No doubt he wished to emphasise his connection with the early family and progenitors of Newton Hall for the purposes of the correspondence.

A photograph from the early 1960s (fig. 35) sheds light on how the building changed in the most recent conversion three decades later. It appears to have lost approximately a quarter of its length, including windows and chimney stacks and part of the one-story extension to the west, which dates from mid-Victorian times. Whilst the reduction in size and change in character is regrettable, the proportions of the diminished building are somewhat more in symmetry. They may also be more in keeping with the original design. The rear elevation of the hall today is in stark though not unsympathetic contrast to the other sides, being faced with plaster rather than with brick. It is hard to know precisely why the property was trimmed in this way and how it reconciled with the listed building status.

The conversion in the 1990s was undertaken in two phases, firstly concentrating on the redevelopment of the hall and then the construction of the seven houses to the rear. It is believed that this second phase was important to the builder in terms of achieving a return on his investment.

Another striking feature of the photograph of the west elevation in the early 1960s is the lack of windows towards the front of the building. This is a throwback to the Window Tax, which was introduced in 1696 and repealed in 1851. Many people reacted against the tax and bricked windows up, giving rise to the expression 'daylight robbery'. We see these windows restored and more dormer windows added in the wake of the 1990s conversion. One of the windows that was in place in the 1960s bore the beguiling inscription, 'Mary Rabet 1797-1799,' in much the same fashion as Catherine Earnshaw's window etchings in *Wuthering Heights*. Nothing further is known about Mary or her raison d'être at Newton Hall.[2]

The brochure advertising the sale in 1963 (fig. 36) is enlightening in a number of respects. The photograph shows the single dormer window to the front, climbing foliage, garages to the right, the low roofs of properties on Plas Newton Lane, and a more elevated wall compared with today behind planted grass verges and the gravel driveway. The hall is hemmed in by mature trees, as it still is. The date and auctioneers are identified and an indication of what might subsequently happen to the estate is given. Inside, the brochure refers to the six self-contained flats — one in the basement, two on the ground floor, two on the first and one on the second — and four flatlets, which were then let on furnished tenancies determinable at short notice. It goes on to add that 'the Hall could be RESTORED TO A PRIVATE RESIDENCE or be further converted for use as a HOTEL, HOSTEL, NURSING HOME or like establishment'. Outline planning consent had been obtained for the area to the west of the fence now in place on that side of the building. It was all set up for change of use. The contents of the hall, which included many fine antiques, were put up for auction.

We now know that, following the sale of the property, the flats were retained and the designated area to the west was developed in the form of the houses that occupy Newton Hall Drive today. It is said that the new owner had wanted to demolish the hall but was prevented from doing so by the preservation order.

In time, the hall became uninhabited and neglected, and Council correspondence from the late 1980s expresses exasperation at its declining condition and the lack of a clear way forward towards restoration. Photographs from the period show the building boarded up, overgrown and crumbling. A Historic England Inspection from June 1992 confirms that the hall was unoccupied and in a poor state of repair. There are multiple references to damage, wear and tear, and vandalism. Children from Kingsway High School, which bordered the estate from 1958 until the school's closure in 2006, often ventured into the grounds, and even into the building itself if they were not too spooked to do so.

It seems that the impasse of the late 1980s and early 1990s was broken with the resolution of an ownership dispute, compulsory purchase by the Council and the selling on to a developer at a fixed price and with a fixed timescale for conversion and sale of the resultant flats. The sales particulars from 'Heritage Homes' from the mid-1990s include a sketch of the hall in its present configuration, with the twelve 'luxury flats' ranging in price from £36,000 to £59,950. It is stated that 'The Hall has now been the subject of an extensive modernisation and refurbishment scheme', which can have been no exaggeration given the condition of the building and its grounds beforehand. What does stretch the bounds of credibility, however, is the further claim that it 'is reputed to have once been the resting place of Charles I'. Whilst this is an alluring concept, we know that Charles was executed in 1649 and that Newton Hall dates from several decades later. He may have passed through Hurleston land on his way into the city on 23rd September 1645, ahead of the Battle of Rowton Heath, but he would not have lodged in Newton if it were not fit habitation for the head of the Hurleston family at that time, let alone the King. Indeed, it is known that, having passed through the East Gate, he stayed two nights at the Lower Bridge Street home of Sir Francis Gamul, a commander in his forces and head of a notable Chester family, before repairing to the relative safety of north Wales after the defeat at Rowton. On his one previous visit to Chester, in September 1642, he would also have been afforded more salubrious accommodation in the city. The claim in the brochure, therefore, may have made the flats more appealing to prospective purchasers, but it has no basis in fact.

The appearance of the hall today and its internal structure have changed little since the 1990s conversion. It is still split into twelve flats, some owner-occupied and some tenanted. The grounds are attractive, compact and well-tended. There is designated parking for residents and visitors to the front of the hall, beyond which are playing fields and buildings belonging to the Creative Campus of Chester University, which took on the site vacated by Kingsway High School. Above the treetops are the historic protuberances of the Lead Shot Tower and the Steam Mill, as well as the broader Chester skyline. Between the 1960s housing and the parking area is a discreet sign which reads 'NEWTON HALL, STRICTLY PRIVATE'. Given the secluded location, incursions are rare and often not unwelcome. Meandering walkers or cyclists occasionally happen upon the building, pausing to absorb the prospect and to muse on its history and incongruity, before returning whence they came.

Conclusion

In some ways, it is impossible to conclude. Like all real-life stories, it defies structure and has a momentum of its own. There is no internal logic and flow, and the people and events that feature do not coalesce into a neat and harmonious whole. At the outset, I described this as a journey, but 'quest' may be a better word. It has been a quest to gather information, to shape it and to share it, rather than towards a single destination. Often, the way has been unsteady and obscure — pock-marked and full of crazy-paving. But it has been worth pursuing, if only to know more about the people who have inhabited the space in which I live and write, stretching back in time. Soon, I will stop writing but Newton Hall will persist and its history will continue to be created. Perhaps in the future another chapter will be written.

What we can do, though, is reflect on what we now know or have been exposed to. Money, which can be a delicate and tawdry subject, is a running theme in the history of Newton Hall. We have seen how the funds were available to build it and, in those turbulent times, could just as easily have been lost. We have seen how money circulates and is augmented within controlled social parameters, through marriage and inheritance. We see old money and new, some of which is corrupted by the most shameful aspects of colonialism. We see money which is hard-earned and we see money which is received gratuitously, often in large amounts over long periods. The sources of money may be assured, offering stability and security, or they may be volatile, threatening ruin and despair.

Bound up with this are the concepts of nobility, civic duty and public service. We have telling insights into the rights and obligations of high office and elevated social status, particularly in the more distant past. But we have kind hearts as well as coronets: for example, in the watchful care of the mysterious Patty, the charitable work of Emma Hesketh and the philanthropy of the Humberstons.

The role of women, their place in society and how little it changed over many centuries is manifest too. Their rights were subordinated to their menfolk, especially within the confines of marriage. A husband may have conferred status and offered the prospect of family life, but at the cost of many freedoms which may otherwise have been enjoyed. Perhaps this is why we have encountered so many 'misses' — women who chose to retain their independence, preserve their assets and make their own way in life.

Inevitably, a history such as this is skewed towards a certain section of society, whose affairs are more amply documented and in whom historians have taken a keener interest. There is a huge but silent undertow of people who have supported the principal occupants of Newton Hall and provided the infrastructure upon which their whole existences were framed. Other than through occasional references in censuses, for example, we have no insight into the lives of mute, inglorious individuals such as these. In their own way, these lives would have been as rich and vibrant as any other, but in detail that is now irretrievably lost.

We have seen people who lived to a ripe old age and people who barely lived at all. High infant mortality was a scourge that spanned the generations and wealth was no buffer against it. We get a glimpse of the heartache associated with this, from the very earliest days of Newton Hall. Some of those who were fortunate enough to survive were marked out by high achievement, enabled by nurture, networks and personal endeavour. On Sir William Parker, for example, we have sufficient information for him to rise a little from the page and take on a three-dimensional form. On others, such as John Nuttall Jr., we have hints at quirks and foibles that we recognise as personality traits in the modern day. There is a timeless quality in the strengths and frailties of the individuals that is reflected in the warp and weft of the building itself. Fortunes have changed, conflicts have raged, decay and destruction have been constant threats, alongside the press of the municipal maw, but Newton Hall still stands to bear witness to the present and the future as well as to so much of our inscrutable past.

Illustrations

Figure 1

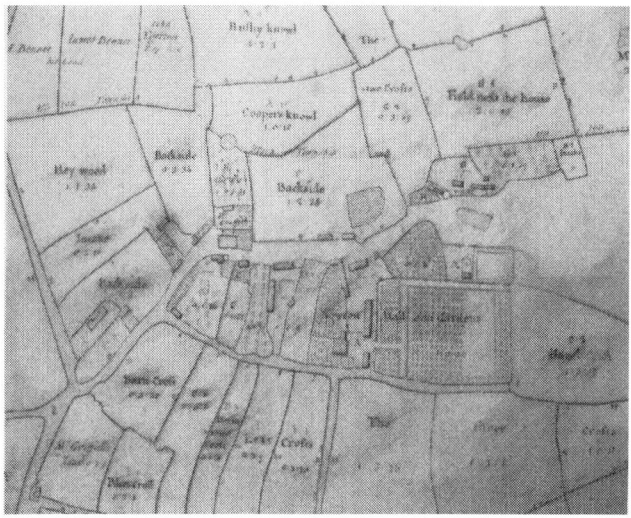

Extract from an estate map of Newton dated 1738

Figure 2

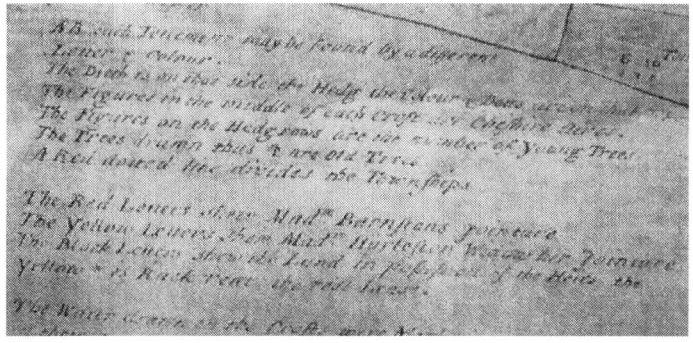

Footnotes to the above map

Figure 3

1988 Spanish Armada Anniversary First Day Cover

Figure 4

St. Peter's Church, Plemstall

Figure 5

Charles Hurleston portrait, Tatton Hall

Figure 6

Hurleston inscription inside St. Peter's Church

Figure 7

Faded tablet commemorating Elizabeth Hurleston, née Lander

Figure 8

Hurleston coat of arms

Figures 9 and 10

Recumbent skeleton motifs on the Hurleston vault at St. Peter's Church

Figure 11

John Needham, tenth Viscount Kilmorey by Gainsborough (circa 1768)

Figure 12

Carden Hall

Figure 13

Grey rectangular stone embedded top right on the Bridge Gate includes 'Henry Hesketh, Murenger' in the inscription from 1782

Figure 14

White building, bottom right, was the location of the Heskeths' wine business (Watergate Street)

Figure 15

Newton House

Figure 16

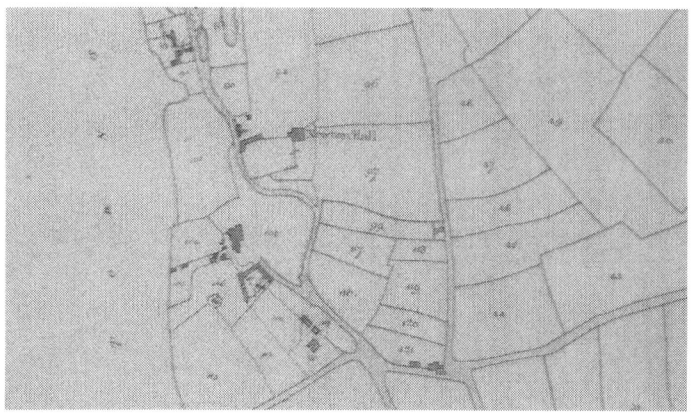

1840 tithe map

Figure 17

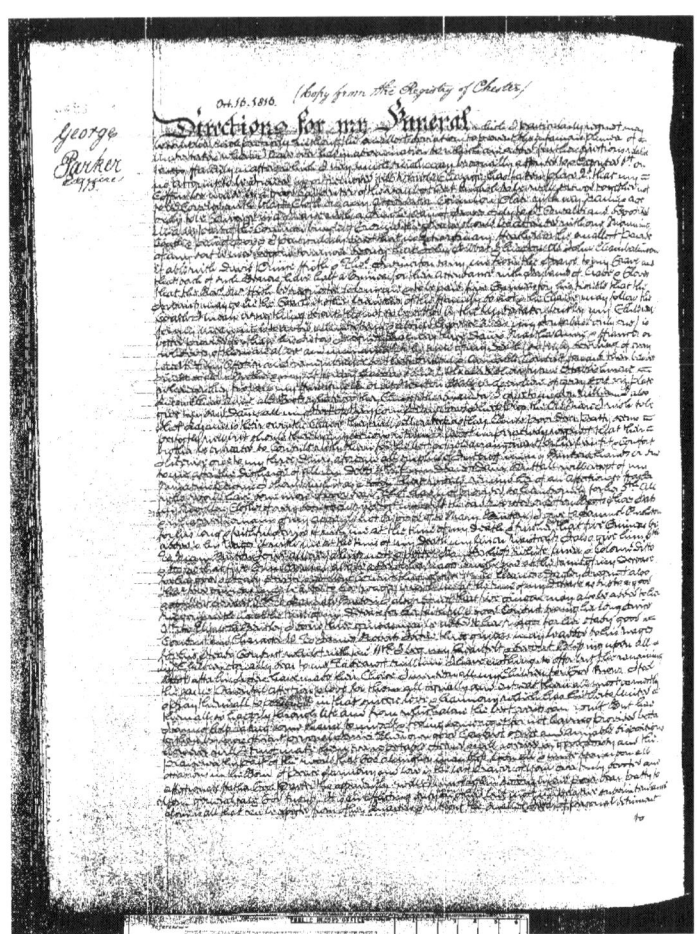

George Parker's will

Figure 18

Sir William Parker (1781–1866), Admiral of the Fleet

Figure 19

Admiral Parker Drive, Shenstone

Figure 20

St. Leonard's Church, Birdingbury

Figure 21

Old Rectory, Birdingbury

Figure 22

George and Mackworth Parker (and Charlie)

Figure 23

Four Humberston-related graves at Holy Ascension Church, Upton, including Anne and Mary together bottom left

Figure 24

Statue of Stapleton Cotton, Viscount Combermere, outside Chester Castle

Figure 25

Reverend George Pearson, 1791–1860

Figure 26

Philip Stapleton Humberston, 19th July 1861, National Portrait Gallery

Figure 27

Reverend Henry Ireland Blackburne, 1826–1903

Figure 28

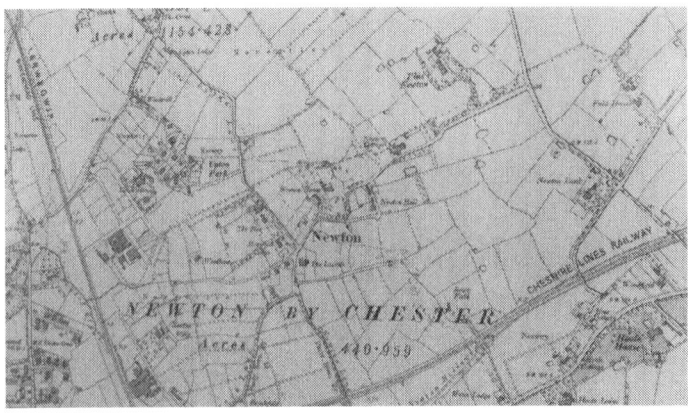

1898 Ordnance Survey map

Figure 29

Boughton Hall, Chester

Figure 30

Alfred and Ida Tyrer

Figure 31

South face of the Eastgate Clock, Chester

Figure 32

Kenney and Rachel Tyrer with an unknown lady

Figure 33

The drive with lime trees, 1950

Figure 34

Newton Hall grounds looking west from the hall, 1950

Figure 35

Newton Hall from the west, 1963

Figure 36

Front cover of 1963 sales brochure

Family Trees

Chapter 1

A. Hurleston fathers and sons

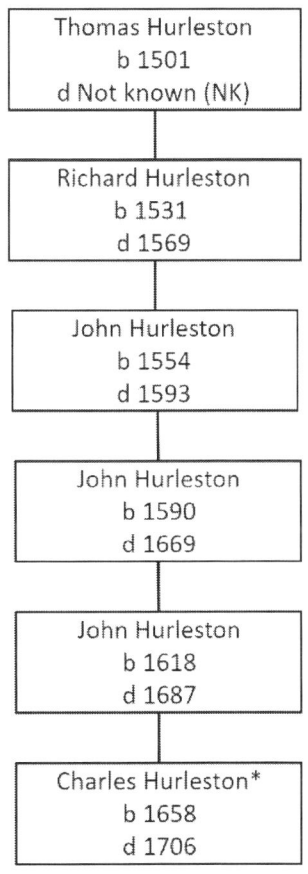

* See Family Tree B

B. Charles Hurleston Sr.'s family

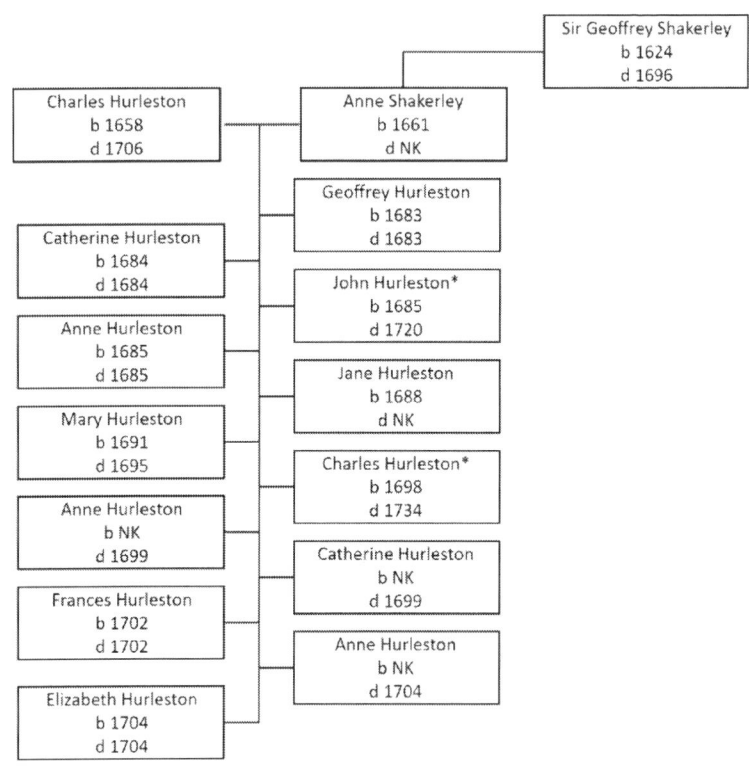

* See Family Tree C

C. John and Charles Hurleston Jr.'s marriages and children

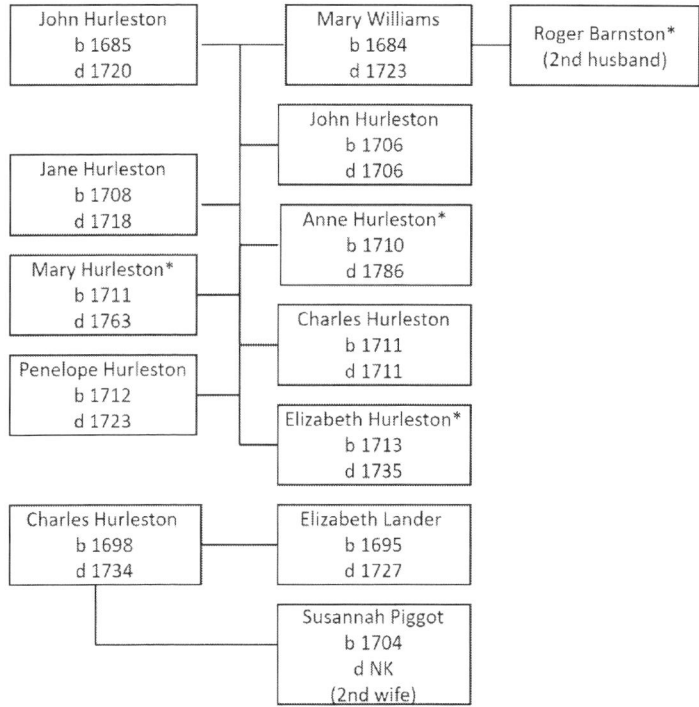

* See Family Tree D

D. Anne, Mary, and Elizabeth Hurleston's marriages

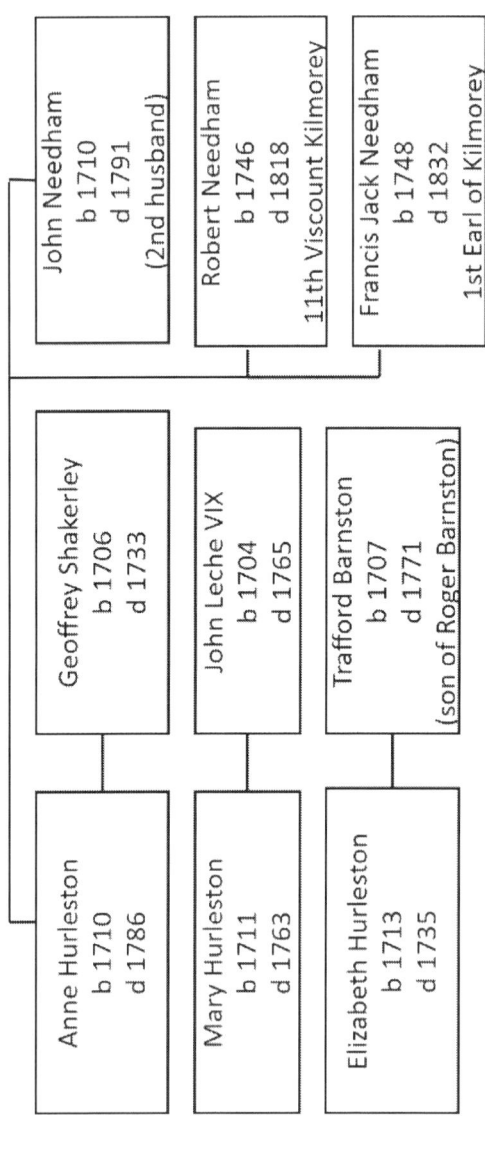

Chapter 3

E. Three generations of the Hesketh family

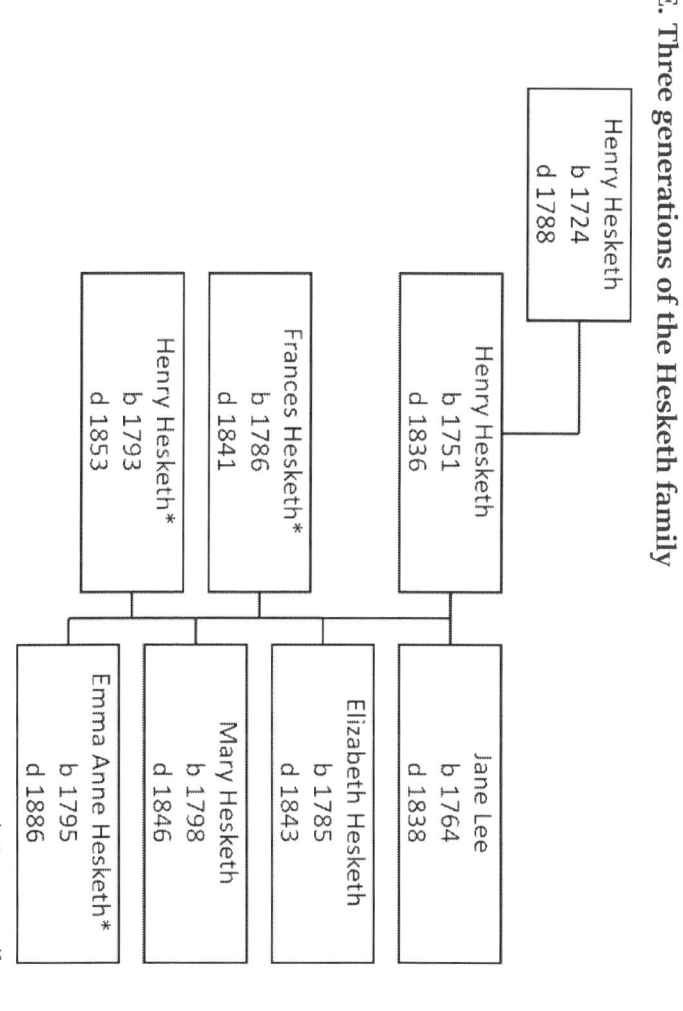

* See Family Tree F

F. Frances, Henry, and Emma Hesketh's marriages

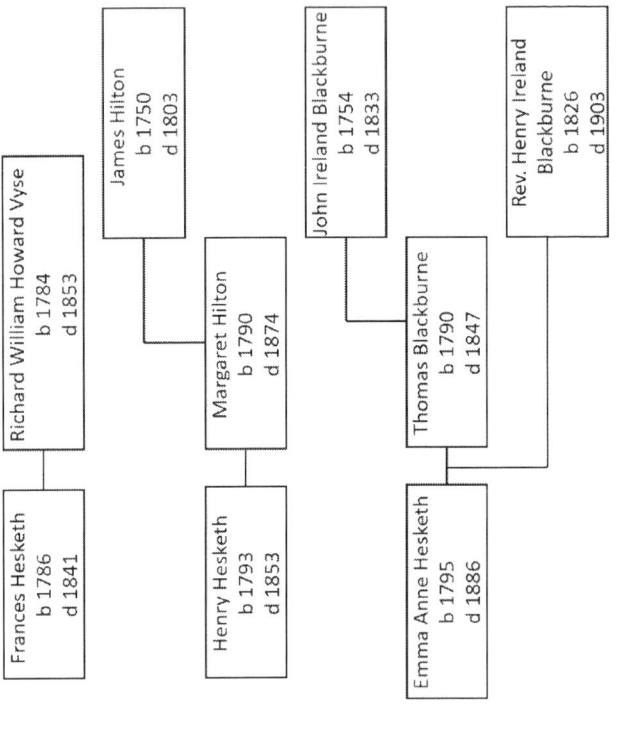

G. George Parker Sr.'s ancestry

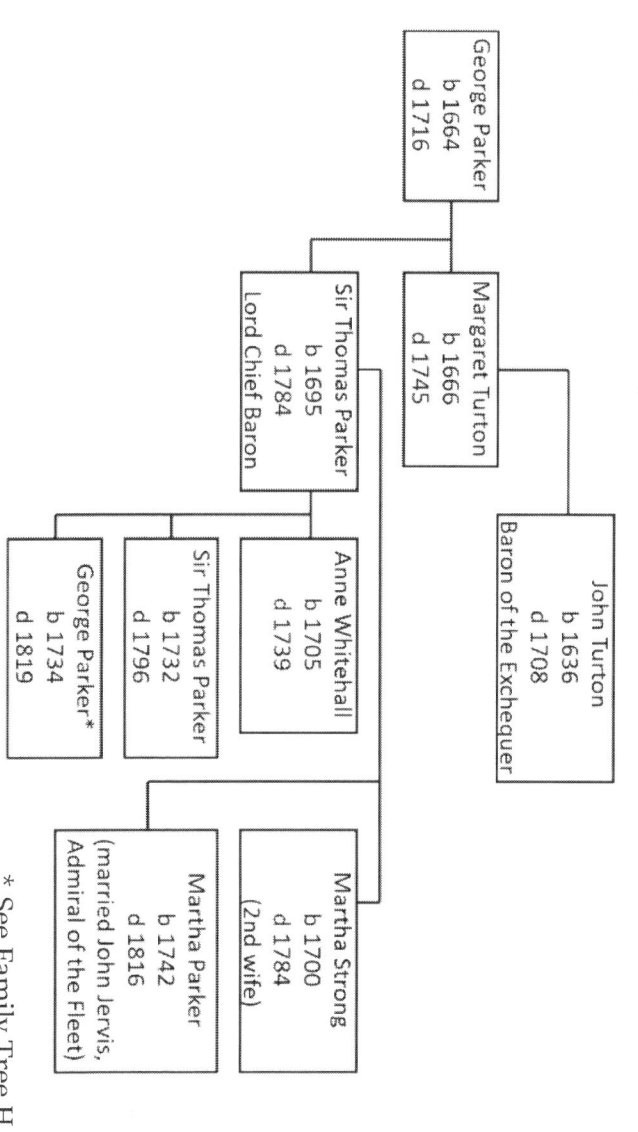

* See Family Tree H

H. George Parker Sr.'s descendants

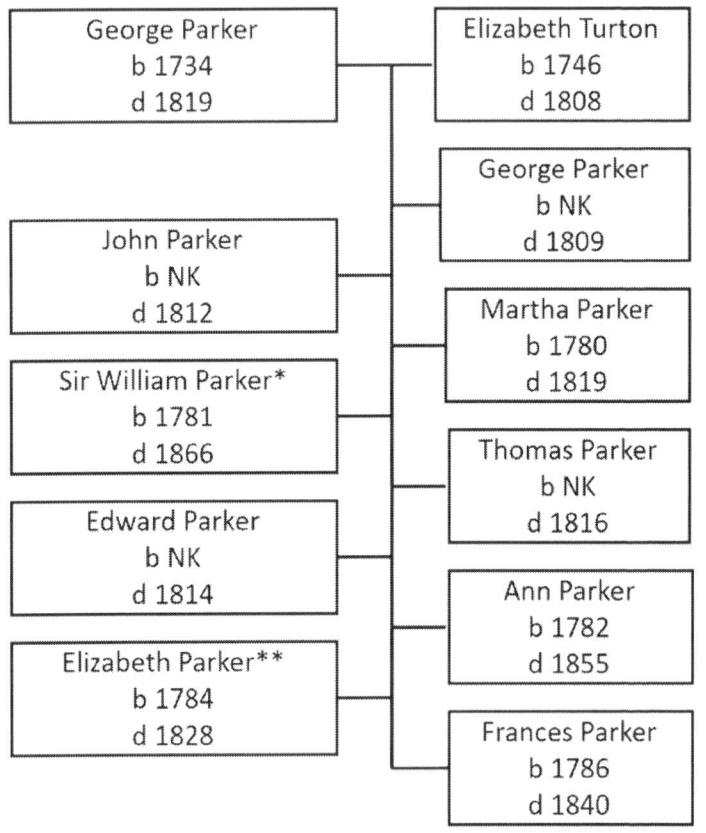

* See Family Tree I
** See Family Tree J

I. Parker and Biddulph connections

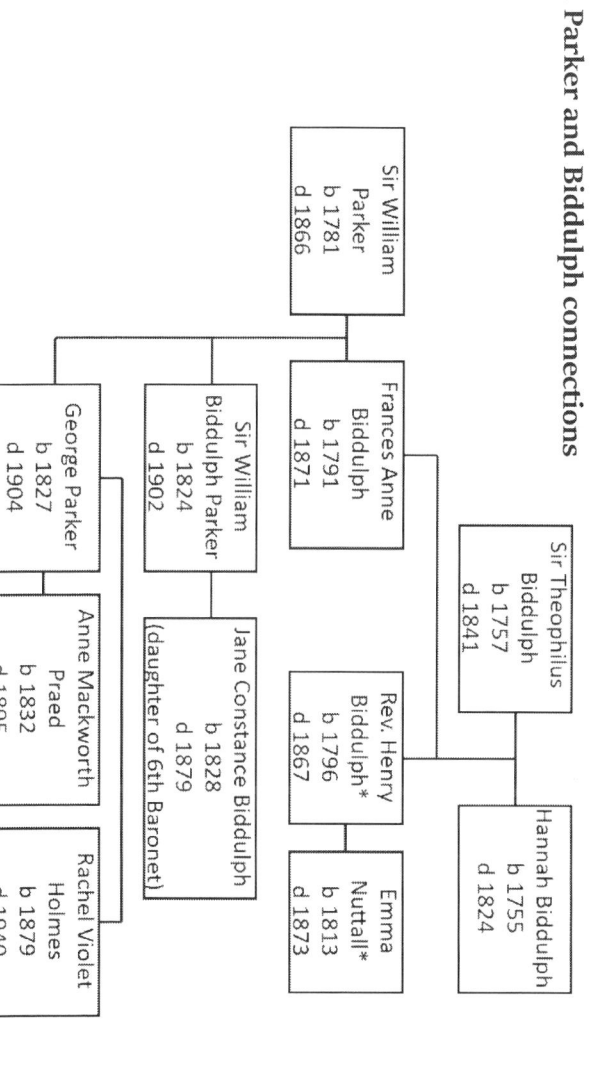

* See Family Tree J

J. Elizabeth Parker's family

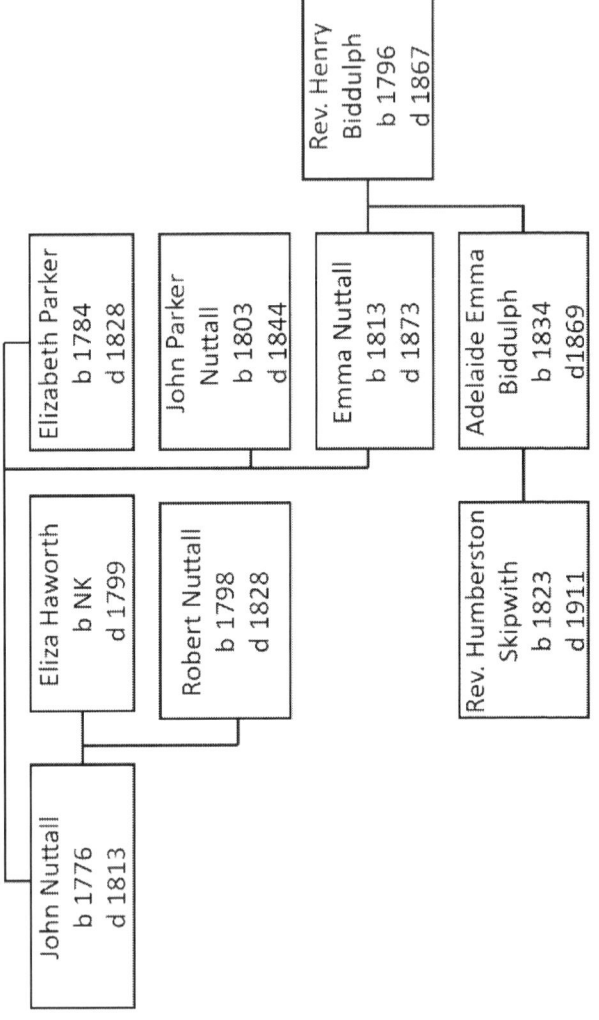

Chapter 4

K. Philip and Catherine Humberston Sr. and their children

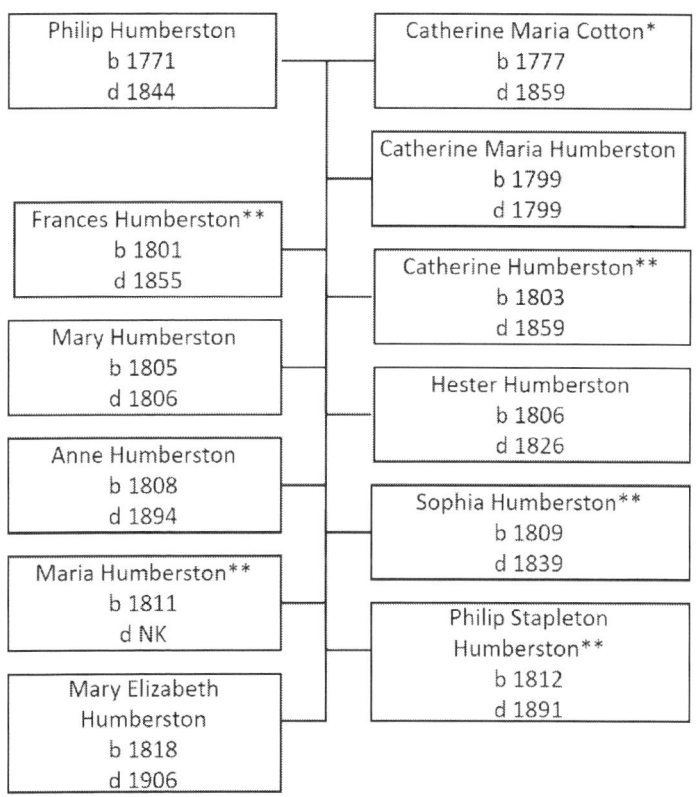

* See Family Tree L
** See Family Tree M

L. Cotton family

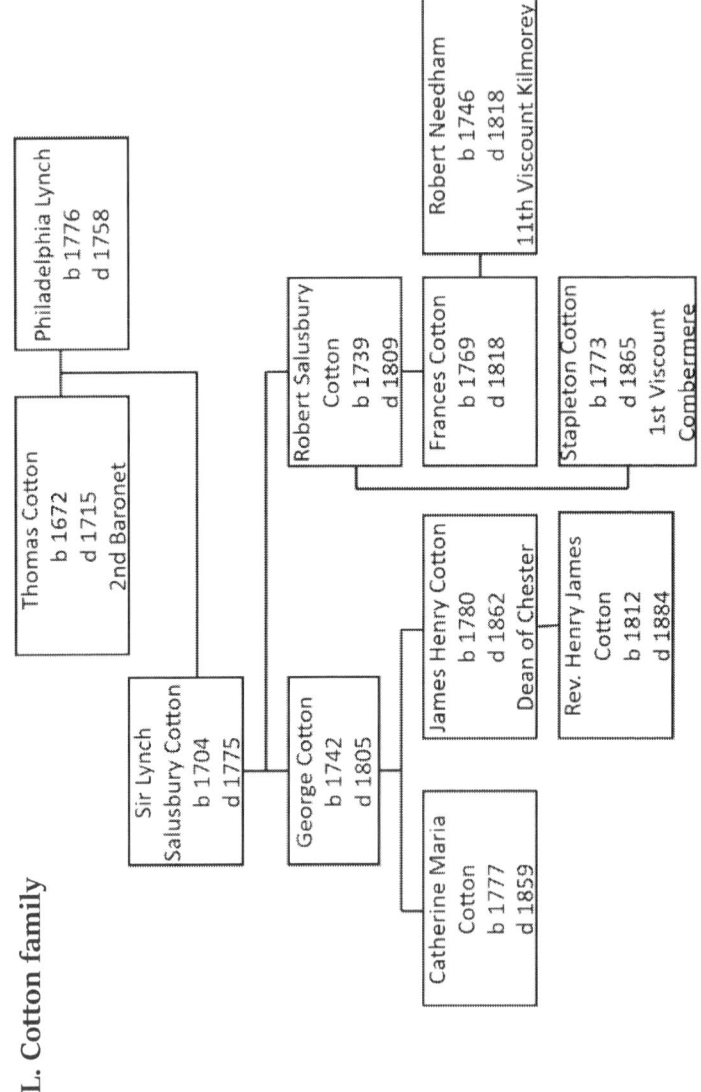

M. Humberston children's marriages

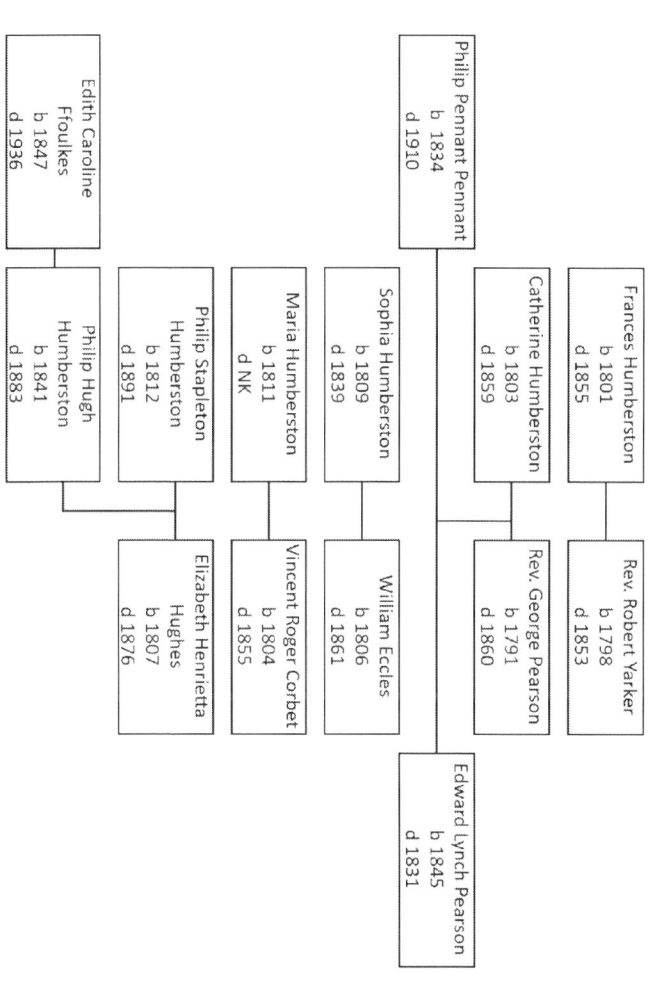

- Frances Humberston b 1801 d 1855 — Rev. Robert Yarker b 1798 d 1853
- Catherine Humberston b 1803 d 1859 — Rev. George Pearson b 1791 d 1860
  - Edward Lynch Pearson b 1845 d 1831
- Sophia Humberston b 1809 d 1839 — William Eccles b 1806 d 1861
- Maria Humberston b 1811 d NK — Vincent Roger Corbet b 1804 d 1855
- Philip Stapleton Humberston b 1812 d 1891 — Elizabeth Henrietta Hughes b 1807 d 1876
  - Philip Hugh Humberston b 1841 d 1883
- Philip Pennant Pennant b 1834 d 1910 — Edith Caroline Ffoulkes b 1847 d 1936

Chapter 5

N. Alfred Tyrer's family

```
William Kenney Tyrer*          Elizabeth Ida Burton
    b 1815                          b 1855
    d 1875                          d 1942
        │                              │
        └──────────────┬───────────────┘
                       │
        ┌──────────────┼──────────────┬──────────────┐
        │              │              │              │
   Alfred Tyrer*  Alfred Kenney    Oliver Tyrer    Ida Tyrer
    b 1849          Tyrer            b 1880         b 1880
    d 1946          b 1878           d 1934         d 1945
                    d 1952                             │
                      │                                │
              Rachel Salkeld                     William Paul
                Robinson                           b 1875
                 b 1882                            d NK
                 d 1952                              │
                                              William E. D. Paul
                                                   b 1916
                                                   d 1940
```

* See Family Tree O

O. 'Kenney' origins

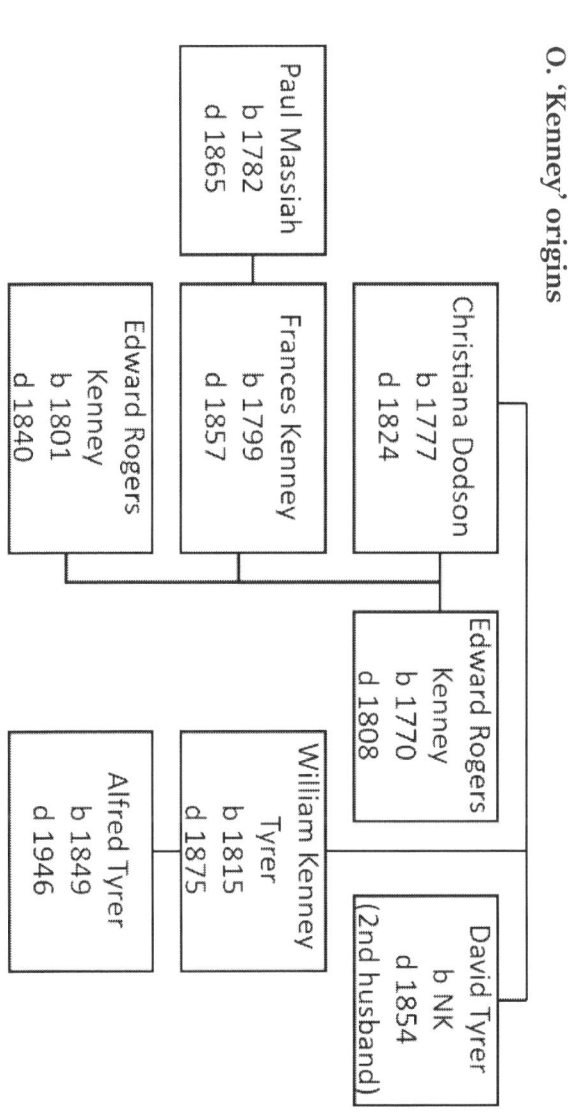

Notes and References

Introduction
1. *Post Office Directory of Chester*, 1878

Chapter 1: The Early History of Newton and Origins of Newton Hall
1. An area in which rights reserved to the monarch have devolved into private hands
2. Approximately thirty acres
3. Shaw, E. G., notes on the history of Newton Hall, Chester (circa 1964)
4. Lewis and Thacker (ed.), *A History of Chester,* Vol. V, p.328 (2005); Ormerod, G., *History of Chester* Vol. 2, pp.772–773 (1816–1819)
5. A person to whom a grant of freehold property is made in feudal law
6. Croston, J., *Nooks and Corners of Lancashire and Cheshire,* pp.318–319 (1982)
7. Ormerod, G., *History of Chester* Vol. 2, pp.772–773 (1816–1819)
8. Jackson, Kenneth Hurleston, letters to Mrs. E. G. Shaw (1956)
9. Wall, B., *Upton-by-Chester* (1984)
10. Visitor information at St. Peter's Church, Plemstall
11. Jackson, Kenneth Hurleston, letters to Mrs. E. G. Shaw (1956)
12. Marshall, P. and Ryrie, A., *The Beginnings of English Protestantism* (2002)

13. *The Victoria History of the County of Chester* Vol. III, Oxford University Press, pp.177–178 (1980)
14. *https://british-history.ac.uk/commons-jrnl/vol5/pp.407-410.*
15. Approx. £160,000 today *http://www.nationalarchives.gov.uk/currency-converter/#currency-result*
16. Jackson, Kenneth Hurleston, letters to Mrs. E. G. Shaw (1956)
17. Ward, S., *Chester — A History*, p.80 (2013)
18. *http://www.chester.shoutwiki.com/wiki/Hoole#Plegmund*
19. *Upton-by-Chester — A People's History,* p.28 (2005)
20. Burke, J., *A Genealogical and Heraldic History of the Commoners of Great Britain and Ireland* Vol. 1 (1835–1838)
21. Barrett, J., *The Great Siege of Chester*, p.99 (2003)
22. A feudal tenure of land involving payment of rent or other non-military service to a superior
23. Jackson, Kenneth Hurleston, Letters to Mrs. E. G. Shaw (1956)
24. *ibid.*
25. *The Cheshire Sheaf*, Vol. 56, p.98
26. Jackson, Kenneth Hurleston, Letters to Mrs. E. G. Shaw (1956)
27. *The Cheshire Sheaf*, Vol. 2 p.20 (written in 1878 based on a document found in the possession of Mr. P. H. Fletcher of Nerquis Hall)
28. *The Cheshire Sheaf*, Vol. 10, p.24 (from 1684)
29. Crossley, F. H., *Cheshire*, p.97 (1949)
30. *The Cheshire Sheaf*, Vol. 24, p.31
31. Morton, E. J., *Old Cheshire Churches*, p.277 (1973) — Plemstall, St. Peter

32. Visitor information boards at St. Peter's Church, Plemstall
33. *https://howardwilliamsblog.wordpress.com/2019/01/20/sex-sin-and-skeletons-on-a-tomb-chest-at-plemstall-cheshire*
34. *The Cheshire Sheaf,* Vol. 34
35. *The Cheshire Sheaf*, Vol. 39
36. Burke, Sir J.B.B., *A Genealogical and Heraldic History of the Extinct and Dormant Baronetcies*, p.546 (1838)
37. Hanshall, J. H., *A History of the County Palatine of Chester*, p.349 (1817)
38. Church of England Parish Records, Corsham, Wiltshire, 1538–1812
39. *https://www.tate.org.uk/art/artworks/gainsborough-john-needham-10th-viscount-kilmorey-n04777*
40. Lewis and Thacker (ed.), *A History of the County of Chester,* Vol. V, Part 2, p.328 (2003)
41. Myllar-Owen, S. (ed.)*, Dictionary of National Biography*, Vol. 1–2 p.156 (1993)
42. *http://chester.shoutwiki.com/wiki/Leche_House*
43. Leach Rixford, E. M., *Families Descended from all the Royal Families in Europe,* p.191 (1932)

Chapter 2: The Property

1. Yorke, T., *British Architectural Styles*, p.21 (2008)
2. Shaw, E. G., notes on the history of Newton Hall, Chester (circa 1964)
3. *https://historicengland.org.uk/listing/the-list/list-entry/1012123*
4. Ormerod, G., *History of the County Palatine and City of Chester,* p.773 (1816–1819)

5. Hanshall, J. H., *A History of the County Palatine of Chester*, p.346 (1817)
6. *ibid.* p.349
7. Hughes, T., *The Vale Royal of England* (1852)
8. *https://www.british-history.ac.uk/statutes-realm/vol6/pp.24-53*
9. Harwell, Hyde, Bubbard, and Pevsner, *The Buildings of England: Cheshire* (2011)

Chapter 3: The Late Eighteenth and Early Nineteenth Century

1. Cheshire Archives and Local Studies, ref. QDD/2/21
2. Bennet, N.R., *The Golden Age of the Port Wine System, 1781 – 1807* (1990)
3. Hemingway, J., *History of the City of Chester from its Foundations to the Present Time* pp.8-9, (1931)
4. A List of Bankrupts with their Dividends, Certificates & c., William Smith and Co, Lombard St, London
5. *http://www.hooleroundabout.com/2018/06/26/flookersbrook-newton-hoole-female-friendly-society/*
6. *Upton-by-Chester—A People's History,* p.74 (2005)
7. The Commercial Directory of Chester 1814–1815 and Pigot's Directory of Cheshire 1822
8. *The Cheshire Sheaf* Vol. 6, 3rd Series pp.8–9
9. *The Cheshire Sheaf 1880* Vol. 2, 1st Series, p.9
10. Stephen, l., and Lee, S., *Dictionary of National Biography*, Vol. 20, p.398 (1909)
11. *https://borthcat.york.ac.uk/index.php/blackburne-emma-anne-nee-hesketh-1795-1886-wife-of-reverend-thomas-blackburne*
12. Duguid, P., University of California, Berkeley, *The Changing of the Guard—British Firms in the Port Trade 1777–1840* (2007)

13. *The Chester Chronicle*, 3rd June 1838
14. *North Wales Daily Post,* 11th September 2019
15. *Hansard,* 22 March 1821, Vol. 4, cc1401–1412
16. *The Cheshire Sheaf*, Vol 8, p.24: *Monumental descriptions of Cheshire Folk in other counties* and Guttridge, G. E., *A Short History of Lichfield Cathedral*, p.82
17. *https://www.search.staffspasttrack.org.uk*
18. *https://englishlocalhistory.wordpress.com/staffordshire-history/the-parker-family-and-park-hall-weston-coyney/*
19. Burke, J., *A Genealogical and Heraldic History of the Commoners of Great Britain*, Vol. 4, p.487 (1833)
20. Moule, T. E., *English Counties Delineated* (1807) and *Magna Britannica* Vol. 2, Part 2 (1810)
21. *http://chester.shoutwiki.com/wiki/Cowper#Overleigh*
22. *http://www3.sympatico.ca/dljordan/parker.htm*
23. Stephen, l., and Lee, S., *Dictionary of National Biography*, Vol. 15 p.289 (1909)
24. Shaw, E. G., notes on the history of Newton Hall, Chester (circa 1964)
25. Phillimore, A., *The Last of Nelson's Captains*, Vol. 3, p.208 (1891)
26. *The Analyst: Quarterly Journal of Science, Literature and the Fine Arts*, Vol. 1, p.74–76 (1834)
27. *http://www.birdingbury.org/*
28. Stamford, Patricia M., *Archaeological Investigations of the Prestwould Slave Quarter, Mecklenburg County, Virginia* (2001)
29. *https://www.genuki.org.uk/big/eng/DEV/Cornwood/CornwoodNotes1918*
30. *Accounts and Papers of the House of Commons*, Vol. 38, p.289 (1838)

31. *National Probate Register*, p.106 (1893)
32. *https://en.wikipedia.org/wiki/George_Ormerod*
33. *http://maps.cheshireeast.gov.uk/tithemaps*

Chapter 4: The Mid- to Late Nineteenth Century

1. *Kelly's Directory*, 1814 and 1822
2. Parsons, J., *History of the Church and Parish of St. Mary on the Hill,* p.56 (1898)
3. Walford, E., *The County Families of the United Kingdom*, p.330 (1884)
4. Legacies of British Slave-ownership: *https://www.ucl.ac.uk/lbs/person/view/2146649293*
5. *https://www.ucl.ac.uk/lbs/person/view/25180*
6. Thackeray, W. M., *The Book of Snobs* (1848)
7. *https://discovery.nationalarchives.gov.uk/details/r/4183ba57-80a1-45b0-8131-a1188ef3efb8*
8. *National Probate Register – Wills*, p.174 (1859)
9. *https://www.genuki.org.uk/big/eng/CHS/chester/chester-christchurch church*
10. *Upton-by-Chester – A People's History*, p.226 (2005)
11. *The Victoria History of the County of Chester*, Vol. III, p.166 (1980)
12. *The Cheshire Sheaf*, Vol.2, p.57 (1880)
13. *The Victoria History of the County of Chester*, Vol. III, p.169 (1980).
14. *https://archives.library.wales/index.php/foulkes-family-of-eriviat*
15. *Upton-by-Chester – A People's History* p.79 (2005)
16. *https://archiveshub.jisc.ac.uk/search/archives*
17. *http://www.hooleroundabout.com/2018/05/21/the-hoole-footbridge-petition/*

18. *https://www.chestercinemas.co.uk/music-hall-history/*
19. *The Cheshire Sheaf*, Vol. 2, 1st Series, p.9 (1880)

Chapter 5: The Early to Mid-Twentieth Century
1. *https://www.cheshire-live.co.uk/news/business/well-known-chester-law-firm-14228450*
2. *http://www.hoolehistorysoc.btck.co.uk/StreetsofHoole/HooleRoad-FollyHouse*
3. *Kelly's Directories* 1919–1920, 1921, and 1923.
4. *http://www.mallandain.com/rf.frost.hills.htm*
5. Barnes, G., *Cheshire History,* No. 42, Millers and Mayors: The Frost family of Chester p.105–115 (2013)
6. *Upton-by-Chester – A People's History*, p.75 (2005)
7. *https://www.ucl.ac.uk/lbs/claim/view/9400*
8. *Upton-by-Chester – A People's History*, pp.74–75 (2005)
9. *ibid.* p.226
10. *Liverpool Echo,* 22nd September, 2015
11. *Upton-by-Chester – A People's History*, p.286 (2005)
12. Shaw, E. G., notes on the history of Newton Hall, Chester (circa 1956)

Chapter 6: Mid-Twentieth Century to the Present Day
1. Shaw, E. G., *notes on the history of Newton Hall, Chester* (circa 1964)
2. *ibid.*

Sources for Illustrations, in order

Extract from an estate map of Newton, 1738. (Private collection)
Footnote to the above map. (Private collection)
John Hurleston, mariner of Chester, on Spanish Armada Anniversary First Day Cover, 1988. (© British First Day Covers)
St. Peter's Church, Plemstall. (Private collection)
Charles Hurleston, circa 1715, artist unknown. (©National Trust, Tatton Park)
Hurleston inscription inside St. Peter's Church, Plemstall. (Private collection)
Tablet commemorating Elizabeth Hurleston (née Lander), outside St. Peter's Church, Plemstall. (Private collection)
Hurleston coat of arms. (©House of Names)
Recumbent skeletons on the Hurleston vault at St. Peter's Church, Plemstall. (Private collection)
John Needham, tenth Viscount Kilmorey, by Thomas Gainsborough. (©Tate Gallery, London)
Carden Hall (©Lost Heritage).
Bridge Gate, Chester, with 'Henry Hesketh, Murenger' inscribed. (Private collection)
Watergate Street, Chester (location of Hesketh's wine business). (Private collection)
Newton House, Chester. (©*Upton-by-Chester—A People's History*)
Tithe map of Newton Hall area, 1840. (Cheshire Archives)

George Parker's last will and testament. (National Archives)

Sir William Parker, date unknown. (Augustus Phillimore, *The Life of Admiral of the Fleet Sir William Parker*)

Admiral Parker Drive, Shenstone, Staffordshire. (Private collection)

St. Leonard's Church, Birdingbury, Warwickshire. (Private collection)

The Old Rectory, Birdingbury, Warwickshire. (©Our Warwickshire)

George and Mackworth Parker, 1875. (©Dartmoor Trust Archive)

Humberston-related graves at Holy Ascension Church, Upton-by-Chester. (Private collection)

Statue of Stapleton Cotton, first Viscount Combermere, outside Chester Castle. (Private collection)

Reverend George Pearson, date unknown. (Private collection)

Philip Stapleton Humberston, 1861. (©National Portrait Gallery, London)

Boughton Hall, Chester. (Cheshire West and Chester Council)

Ordnance Survey map of Newton area, 1898. (Private collection)

Alfred and Ida Tyrer, date unknown. (©Chester Wiki)

Eastgate Clock, Chester. (Private collection)

Kenney and Rachel Tyrer, date unknown. (Private collection)

Newton Hall driveway, 1950. (Private collection)

Newton Hall grounds looking west, 1950. (Private collection)

Newton Hall from the west, 1963. (Private collection)

Newton Hall sales brochure cover, 1963. (Private collection)

Index

Abbey of St. Werburgh, 3-4
Alexandra Park, 96, 104
All Saints Church, 86
American War of Independence, 26, 53, 74
Anne, Queen, v, 14, 28-29, 31, 37
Bache, 10, 83, 115
Barnston, 23-25, 42, 113-115
    John, 24
    Roger, 23
    Trafford, 23-24, 113
Bhurtpore, Siege of, 80
Biddulph, 61-62, 65-69, 73
    Adelaide Emma, 65
    Rev. Henry, 65, 67, 69
    Sirs Theophilus, 61, 67
Birdingbury, 61, 65, 67-68
Blackburne, 48, 86
    Rev. Thomas, 48-49, 86
    Rev. Henry Ireland, 86
Bodfari, 94
Boot, Robert, 122
Boughton Hall, 105-106, 115
Brereton, Sir William, 8, 11, 18
Bristol, 81
Brown, 56, 94, 101, 104
    Anne, 101
    Charles, 104
    George, 94
    William, 101

Browns of Chester, 56, 74, 95
Butler, Eleanor, 45
Carden Hall, 27, 117-118
Castle Camps, Cambridgeshire, 83, 90
Charles I, King, 9, 26, 32, 48, 127
Charles II, King, 9, 15, 30
Chartist Movement, 75
Cheshire Regiment, 88, 97, 119
Chester Book Club, 88
Chester Castle, 12, 18, 72, 80, 85
Chester Cathedral, 42, 49, 54, 87-88
Chester Courant, The, 42, 112
Chester Music Hall, 100
Chester Railway Station, 74, 94
Chester Zoo, 110
Civil War, 7, 10, 14, 23-24, 33, 36, 52, 58, 88
Colston, Edward, 81
Colwyn, 50
Corbet, 83-84, 93, 97
    Robert St. John, 93
    Vincent Roger, 83-84
Cotton, 4-5, 70, 79-82
    Henry James, 82
    Sir George, 5, 79-80
    Sir Lynch Salusbury, 79
    Sir Robert Salusbury, 80
    Stapleton (first Viscount Combermere), 80-82
Cowper, Thomas, 58
D-Day, 120
Dickens, Charles, 100
Dicksons' Nurseries, 95
Dissolution of the Monasteries, 4-5, 7, 79
Douglas, John, 88

Douro, River, 40, 50
Earl Haig, 106
Eastgate Clock, 110
Edward VII, King, 96
Edward VIII, King, 120
Elizabeth I, Queen, 5, 24, 57
Eriviatt Hall, 90-91
Ermine, 21, 42, 122
Eton College, 87, 114
Evans Lloyd, Edward, 110, 115
Evill, F., 108
Falmouth, 92
Fairbanks, Douglas Jr., 119
Fenian Plot, 88
Ffoulkes, 90-91, 98, 115
    Cecilia, 98
    Constance, 98
    Edith Caroline, 90-91, 98
    John Jocelyn, 90
Flookersbrook, 10-11, 21, 35-36, 42, 64, 104
Folly House, 104
French Revolution, 26, 74
Frost, 105-108, 115, 119, 121
    Francis Aylmer, 105
    James Garrett Sr., 105
    James Garrett Jr., 106
    Jane, 105
    Margaret, 105-107
    Robert, 105
    Sir John, 107
Gamul, Sir Francis, 127
George I, King, 19, 29
George III, King, 26, 75

George IV, King, 75
Georgetown, British Guiana, 109
Glan-y-Wern, 93, 97
Glorious Revolution, 29
Grand National, 112
Great Fire of London, 30
Great Reform Act, 75, 80
Grosvenor Bridge, 74, 85
Grosvenor family, 4-5, 19, 22, 24, 28, 58, 88
Grosvenor Museum, 100
Grosvenor Park, 100
Gwersyllt, Denbighshire, 79
Halle, Charles, 100
Harrison, James, 87
Helps, Thomas, 86, 106, 110
Henley, 106
Hesketh, 39-51, 59, 64, 72-73, 75, 86, 130
    Elizabeth, 47,
    Emma, 42, 46, 48-49, 64, 130
    Frances, 46, 48
    Henry (b 1724), 39-40
    Henry (b 1751), 39-43, 45-46, 50
    Henry (b 1793), 41, 45, 50-51
Historic England, 36-37, 126
Holy Trinity Church, 40
Hoole, 37, 42, 64, 86, 94, 96, 101, 104-105, 116, 120
Hughes, 83, 89, 115
    Edward, 89
    Elizabeth, 83, 89-90
    Hugh Robert, 89
Humberston, 67-69, 76-79, 81-94, 96-101, 104, 107, 115, 123, 130
    Anne, 76, 78-79, 84, 91, 94, 97-98

    Catherine (b 1777), 77-78
    Catherine (b 1803), 77-78
    Mary, 84, 91-93, 97, 104
    Philip, 77
    Philip Hugh, 87, 91-93, 98
    Philip Stapleton, 78, 83-91, 93-94, 97
Hurleston, 4-25, 27-36, 58, 71-72, 79, 81, 113, 118
    Anne (daughter of John, b 1685), 79
    Anne (wife of John, b 1590), 17, 81
    Charles, 12-14, 18-25, 35-36, 39
    Dorothy, 10
    Dr. John, 6
    Elizabeth, 22-23, 28, 113
    John (b 1554), 6-7
    John (b 1590), 7-11, 123
    John (b 1618), 7-11, 13-15, 17, 19-20, 35
    John (b 1685), 18-21, 23
    Mary, 27-28, 72, 118
    Penelope, 23, 27
    Peter, 123
    Richard, 5-7, 57
Huskisson, William, 49
Jackson, Kenneth Hurleston, 123-124
Jacobite Rising, 18
Jervis, John, 53, 60
Kempe, Charles Eamer, 90
Kilmorey, 26, 39, 42-43, 52, 72, 81, 95, 104
    tenth Viscount, 26, 81
    eleventh Viscount, 81
    twelfth Viscount/first Earl, 26
Kingsway, 32-33, 126-127
Kinmel Hall, 89
Lead Shot Tower, 73, 127

Leche, 25, 27-28, 72, 118
Lichfield, 48, 51-53, 61-62, 67, 69, 82, 87
Linden Grove, Queens Park, 99, 105
Logan, 110, 113
    Edward, 110
    Roland, 113
Lower Bridge Street, 28, 127
Lusitania, 112
Mackworth Praed, 69
    Anne Elizabeth, 69
    William, 69
Manchester Cathedral, 57
Marlborough, Duke of, 29
Massiah, Paul, 109
Mickle Trafford, 6
Mollington, 85-86, 92-94, 97, 103, 115
Monmouth, Duke of, 15, 17-18
Morgan, Bill, 111, 116
Nantlys, 93-94
Napoleon, Emperor, 49, 53-54, 73
Needham (See 'Kilmorey'), 26-27, 81
Nelson, Lord, 61
Newton Cottage, 101, 107
Newton House, 43-44, 101
Nuttall, 5, 55, 57-58, 66, 131
    Emma, 55-56, 58-59
    John, 5, 55, 57-58, 131
    John Parker, 66
Overleigh Hall, 58
Park Hall, Staffordshire, 52-53
Parker, 44, 51-53, 56-70, 72-73, 75, 77, 80, 82, 84, 91, 131
    Ann, 66, 68-69
    Edward, 53-54, 80

  Elizabeth (b 1746), 52
  Elizabeth (b 1784), 57
  Frances, 65, 72
  George (b 1664), 52
  George (b 1734), 52-61
  George (b 1827), 65, 69-70
  Martha, 54, 60, 64
  Sir Thomas (b 1695), 53
  Sir Thomas (b 1732), 53
  Sir William, 54-55, 60-66, 69-70, 131
Parys Mine Company, 89
Pearson, 83-85, 87-88, 94, 97-98
  Edward Lynch, 98, 176
  George, 83-84, 87
  James Falconer, 85
Pennant, 12, 93-94, 97-98
  David, 94
  Philip Pennant, 93-94, 97-98
Phillimore, Sir Augustus, 62
Picton Hall, 6, 11, 14, 17
Piggot, 22
  Robert, 22
  Susannah, 22
Pindar, Sir Peter, 9, 10, 16
Plas Newton, 43-44, 109-112, 114, 125
Polo, 112, 114
Ponsonby, Sarah, 45
Pyramids of Giza, 48
Roberts, 110
  Benjamin Chaffers, 110
  Robert, 110
Roodee, The, 112
Rowton Heath, Battle of, 11, 127

Royal Agricultural Show, 96
Rupert, Prince, 11
Scott, George Gilbert, 100
Sedgemoor, Battle of, 15
Shakerley, 12, 18, 20, 23, 25-26, 79
    Geoffrey, 12, 18, 23, 25, 79
    Sir Geoffrey, 12, 23, 26
Shavington Hall, 27
Shaw, 122-123
    George Edward, 122
    Elizabeth, 122
Shenstone, 61-62, 77, 82
Skipwith, 68-69, 77
    Francis, 69
    Rev. Humberston, 68-69
    Sir Grey, 68
Slavery, 79-81, 109
Smith, Cecil, 103-104
Spanish flu, 120
Stanley Palace, 41
Stapleton, 81
    James Russell, 81
    Catherine, 81
St. Bridget's Church, 85
St. John's Church, 86-87, 100
St. Mary's on the Hill Church, 78, 85-86
St. Olave's Church, 87
St. Oswald's Church and Parish, 13-14, 54, 60, 86
St. Peter's Church, Plemstall, 17, 19-20, 23, 71, 86, 123
Steam Mill, 105, 127
Stevenson's *Rocket*, 48-49
Stretton Hall, 118
Stuart, James Francis Edward, 18

Stubbs, William, Bishop of Chester, 106
Tatton Hall, 19
Thackeray, W. M., 81
Thomas, Faithful, 71-72
Townshend, Charles, 70-71, 82, 95
Trafalgar, Battle of, 61, 74
Tremeirchion, 94
Turton, John, 51-52
Tyrer, 108-119, 121-122
    Alfred, 109-113
    Alfred Kenney, 108, 109, 112, 114-118
    Christiana, 108
    David, 108
    Ida, 111, 117
    Oliver, 113-114
    Rachel, 108, 114-116, 118
    William Kenney, 108
University of Chester, 33, 127
Upton-by-Chester, 71, 86, 92, 113, 116
    Cockpit, 87
    Golf Club, 71, 86
    Holy Ascension Church, 82, 86, 89, 92-93, 97-98, 107, 110, 114
    Local History Group, *iv*
    Mill, 87
    St. Mary's School, 92
    Upton Lawn, 86, 106-107, 110, 115
    Victoria Hotel, 87
    War Memorial, 113
Vyse, Richard, 48
Wall Street Crash, 120
Watergate Street, 27, 40-41
Waterloo, Battle of, 67, 74

Wellington, Duke of, 24, 49, 54, 81
Whitefriars, 77, 79, 85-86
William II, Prince of Orange, 9
William III, King, 29
William IV, King, 75
Wordsworth, William, 45, 51
Yarker, Rev. Robert, 83

About Atmosphere Press

Atmosphere Press is an independent, full-service publisher for excellent books in all genres and for all audiences. Learn more about what we do at atmospherepress.com.

We encourage you to check out some of Atmosphere's latest releases, which are available at Amazon.com and via order from your local bookstore:

The Swing: A Muse's Memoir About Keeping the Artist Alive, by Susan Dennis
Possibilities with Parkinson's: A Fresh Look, by Dr. C
Gaining Altitude - Retirement and Beyond, by Rebecca Milliken
Out and Back: Essays on a Family in Motion, by Elizabeth Templeman
Just Be Honest, by Cindy Yates
You Crazy Vegan: Coming Out as a Vegan Intuitive, by Jessica Ang
Detour: Lose Your Way, Find Your Path, by S. Mariah Rose
To B&B or Not to B&B: Deromanticizing the Dream, by Sue Marko
Convergence: The Interconnection of Extraordinary Experiences, by Barbara Mango and Lynn Miller
Sacred Fool, by Nathan Dean Talamantez
My Place in the Spiral, by Rebecca Beardsall
My Eight Dads, by Mark Kirby

About the Author

Chris Fozzard is a teacher and local historian. He has conducted research into local history for many years and uses this as the basis for providing walks and talks in his local area. *A Short History of Newton Hall, Chester* is his first foray into writing extensively about the subject.

Printed in Great Britain
by Amazon